Political Correctness and Public Finance

D1614749

Dennis O'Keeffe
University of North London

with a Foreword by
Andrew Neil

Published by the IEA Education and Training Unit
1999

First published in December 1999 by
The Institute of Economic Affairs
2 Lord North Street
Westminster
London SW1P 3LB

Printed in Great Britain by
Hartington Fine Arts Limited, Lancing, West Sussex
Set in Century Schoolbook and Bookman Old Style

Contents

Foreword

The proposition is so simple, even obvious, yet pregnant with profound implications for our education system, that it is remarkable how little it has been discussed. Put bluntly, Dennis O'Keeffe argues that much of what ails our schools and universities can be traced to the fact that the state is the dominant supplier of their funds.

The state's virtual monopoly of education has led directly to the appalling standards in so many of our schools, which particularly blight the life-chances of the most underprivileged children, and to what he dubs the 'ideological fanaticism in education' which masquerades in the many manifestations of political correctness now gripping our universities in a debilitating left-wing McCarthyism.

O'Keeffe believes that these blots on the educational land-scape on both sides of the Atlantic could be eliminated, or at least reduced, if education was more open to market mechanisms. It is a compelling thesis: state monopolies have proved inadequate providers in everything from steel to supermarkets. It stands to reason that they are not much good at the provision of education either.

Parents would hardly put up with teachers who cannot impart to their children the basics of numeracy and literacy if they had directly to stump up for the teachers' salaries themselves. Students would not put up with third-rate lecturers and substandard courses in which the nostrums of PC over-rule the natural free spirit of learning and inquiry if they had a wider choice and better possibilities than those currently on offer from the state monopoly.

Perhaps the most important part of O'Keeffe's work is the way he lays bare the educational mindset which results from the state's near-monopoly of schools and universities. It is more than just the usual triumph of producer self-interest over the consumer, though that is apparent every time a spokesperson for a teaching union opens his or her mouth.

More fundamentally, those who depend entirely on the state for their resources become hostile to markets and private finance, which they see as a threat to their settled ways and privileges. Just as the BBC produces so many journalists naturally hostile to market mechanisms because they work for a state-financed broadcaster, so state education is dominated by a nomenklatura steeped in collectivist culture.

The author's call for a revitalised 'sociology of knowledge' to explain and document the link between under-performance, extremist ideology and the monopoly provision of education by the state should be heeded if we are to fill one of today's neglected academic voids and improve our education system in the process.

The problem is that so much shoddy academic discourse is still dominated by the notion that education is a reflection of capitalist society when the fact is that, even within societies as free-market as America, education remains one of the last redoubts of socialist central planning, in which choice and diversity for the overwhelming majority of parents and students are alien concepts.

There should be no mystery why, despite the renaissance in market solutions these past 20 years, education remains soaked in socialist ideas. While the left has lost so many of the economic arguments, it has regrouped to fight for socialism in social policy.

In what young German Marxists of the Sixties used to call the 'long march through the institutions', PC socialism has succeeded in scaling the commanding heights of our society: social workers, teachers, even police chiefs and judges are now imbued with this ideology. The market may have triumphed in economics but the collectivist left has won many of the social arguments.

As a result, what O'Keeffe describes as 'sectoral socialism' still dominates even in flourishing market economies. In education, this has been a wholly taxpayer-financed takeover, even though it has operated against the interests of the majority of taxpayers.

How to change that is more difficult than identifying the problem and its causes. Our culture remains steeped in the notion that only the state can provide educational opportunity for the many, even though the evidence increasingly accumulates that a state-dominated education has become a barrier to social mobility. Those who read Dennis O'Keeffe's work, however, will come away with a better understanding of the fundamental reasons for the failure of our education system. He has provided the essential first step to progress.

August 1999   ANDREW NEIL
                                Publisher of Press Holdings Ltd

Biographical note

Dennis O'Keeffe MA, PhD is Senior Lecturer in Sociology of Education at the University of North London. He is a specialist in the Sociology and Economics of Education and has published widely on matters of social theory and education in British and American journals. His critique of British teacher education, *The Wayward Elite*, was published by the Adam Smith Institute in 1990. His innovating study of truancy, *Truancy in English Secondary Schools*, was published by HMSO in 1994. He also specialises in translating social scientific literature from French. At present he is translating Benjamin Constant's *Principes de politique*.

Acknowledgements

I am greatly indebted to the Earhart Foundation and in particular to David Kennedy and Tony Sullivan for the Foundation's generous provision of financial assistance in the writing of this book. I must also sincerely thank the University of North London for freeing up my timetable to facilitate the writing. I am very grateful to John Blundell, General Director of the IEA and to Andrew Turner of the IEA Education and Training Unit, for their good offices in liaising between the Foundation and the University.

Very many friends and colleagues helped with the ideas in this book. I cannot name them all, but I must express my especial gratitude to James Tooley, David Marsland, Andrew Turner, Gerry Frost, Tony Flew, Ken Minogue, Digby Anderson, David Levy, Roger Scruton, Merrie Cave, Jacques Garello, Helen Szamuely, Nick Capaldi, Wayne Shute, Bruce Cooper, Michael Aeschliman, Peter Mullen, John Wilkinson, and Michael Conolly. My students at the University of North London were always ready with useful critical advice. My son Matthew was helpful on the overall argument. Finally, and most of all, I must thank my wife Mary for her unfailingly perceptive commentary.

London
May 1999

Between craft and credulity the voice of reason is stifled.
Edmund Burke

Author's note

This work is interdisciplinary in character. Some readers may find the short glossary on non-economic terms included useful. The first use of all such terms is signalled in the text by the use of **bold type**.

1 | Corruption and the academy: an overview

Introduction

This short book looks at a neglected topic: the links between ideological extremism and public finance. Ideological extremism is a form of **antinomian** corruption, in which standards of argument and evidence are lowered and subverted. Extremist ideas about the nature of our society, about relations between races and sexes, about culture and intelligence, about history and morality, are now commonplace in the universities and even some of the primary and secondary schools of countries like Britain and America.

Indeed, these ideas are common in all the advanced societies that have populations mainly of European race and Christian background. Such ideas, this work will argue, are mostly runaway outgrowths of the protean idea of equality. Equality having been for good or ill the defining notion of twentieth-century social thought, it would be quite possible to mount a thoroughgoing study of intellectual extremism on a detailed international basis. That the focus in this book is on America and Britain is mainly a matter of convenience. Their education systems are rather alike and, with the coming of mass higher education to Britain, becoming more so. Although some critics might want to stress various contrasts between their main educational arrangements, so close are these in the two key respects of heavy reliance on public finance and the pervasive presence of egalitarian ideology, that differences of specific detail seem as nothing by comparison. This book is centrally concerned with an undeniable common obsession in matters educational: the American and British addiction today to certain ideas which most citizens would see as outlandish.

These ideas – at times concerted campaigns – are widely deplored, though by definition there are also many interested parties who defend and publicise them vociferously. Little has been said, however, about how such exponents have contrived to spread and sustain these ideas in the face of so much public hostility or indifference.

There is a relatively easy and obvious explanation available, though one surprisingly little explored. Most schooling in the free societies is publicly financed and provided by local or central government bodies. Most tertiary study too, is financed by the taxpayer. The routine education of most of our young people takes place outside the market system most economists see as essential to economic efficiency. The easiest way to understand the growth of ideological fanaticism in education is to see it as an outcome of the suppression of markets. Just as nationalised industries usually produce sub-standard goods, so publicly financed education too tends to low-quality production. Ideological extremism is one of the *forms* taken by this low quality. Reliance on public finance and state provision denies people the competition markets generate and the exits they offer to dissatisfied customers. It also hugely enhances the discretion of the suppliers. The less producers have to consult consumers, the more likely they are to do as they please. The results of a captive and disenfranchised clientèle in the case of education include low standards of cognitive and intellectual competence *and* a related flourishing of ideological excesses. Easier exit would have served to correct both these results.

Ideological excesses are not, of course, confined to places of learning. They affect the media, the social services and even private commerce. But education is their main redoubt. Many educational personnel see their main function as engaging in egalitarian social engineering. For decades many universities have been obsessed with 'equality' in all its protean guises, up to and including the fantastical ideas and practices now known as 'political correctness' (PC).

This phenomenon of PC is easier to recognise than to define, since as the next chapter will show, it is neither unitary in overall terms nor stable substantively. At its core, however, PC is the modern cult of equality, now that the Marxist war between labour and capital has been largely abandoned. For the old class antagonisms, PC now substitutes conflicts of race, sex, culture and sexual orientation. Quotidian and intellectual relationships alike have been affected across a very wide range of human affairs. It is asserted that there are correct and incorrect ways of thinking, speaking, walking, talking and interrelating,

15

especially in matters of race, sex and culture. It is alleged that power in the past upheld inequalities whose overthrow a reconstituted power must now secure.

What has to be most emphatically noted in any preliminary account, however, is not just the substantive content of PC – bizarre though it usually is – but the wholly unforeseen hatred and fanaticism which this contemporary form of an ancient obsession has summoned up. It is the psychological atmosphere of PC which most immediately calls to mind its totalitarian connections, though there are strong ideological likenesses too, as we shall argue.

The real question is how so strange a set of developments could appear at all in free societies like the USA and Britain. Most people are either embarrassed by or straightforwardly hostile to them. We have, therefore, to ask how they could arise. There is a vast literature on PC and its constantly multiplying and changing contributory currents; but there is remarkably little on the financial sustenance of wayward ideologies, a gap all the stranger in that other social and moral ills have been advisedly linked with public funds.

Who pays the piper calls the tune

The old adage has it that 'he who pays the piper calls the tune'. This decisive power of the purchaser is an obvious feature of commercial transactions, and of any economic order mostly based on commerce. Such consumer sovereignty is the core of economic efficiency.[1]

Public finance has quite opposite economic implications. Extensive writings have shown how public finance promotes economic *inefficiency*, the work of Friedman in America[2] and of Seldon in Britain[3] being just some of the better-known examples, and confirmed by an obdurate international evidence. There is

---

1 The 'Consumer is King' idea popularised by Samuelson's famous textbook still has great explanatory force. Paul A. Samuelson *Economics: An Introductory Analysis*, N.Y.: McGraw Hill, 1961.
2 Milton Friedman *Capitalism and Freedom,* University of Chicago Press, 1962. Friedman's corpus is enormous, but this now famous book remains the classical statement of the freedom/capitalism link.
3 Arthur Seldon *The Dilemma of Democracy: The Political Economics of Over-Government*, Hobart Paper 136, Institute of Economic Affairs, 1998. This is the latest in a long line of works celebrating the efficiency and benevolence of the free market.

now, indeed, no room for doubt: private enterprise is much more efficient than state production.[4] The latter, whether this implies the old Soviet-type economies or public sector activity within predominantly market systems, is marked by radical producer-capture and disenfranchisement of consumers. For example, E.G. West has alleged of education in the British case that since 1870 it has been taken over by 'politicians, bureaucrats and rent-seekers'.[5]

Many of the ills of producer-capture in certain sectors of otherwise market-based economies are quite familiar. In Britain and America illiteracy and innumeracy are clearly associated with lack of competition and exit in schools. This is what educational vouchers are for; to facilitate exit and choice, and to enforce competition.[6] State-generated welfare dependency, too, has adverse moral and social effects. Handouts weaken everyday values, a well-known debilitation which should also be recognised itself as a form of economic inefficiency.[7] Similarly,

---

4 Despite some vague talk about the 'third way', few reputable economists even try to deny the superiority of markets now. Whatever the belief in the public sector now, it is not theorised in economic terms. It is mostly a sentimental attachment.

5 In other words it has been subject to producer-capture: E. G. West 'Education Without the State' in Arthur Seldon (ed.) *Reprivatising Welfare After the Lost Century*. Institute of Economic Affairs, 1996, p.19. Producer-capture is fundamentally the same phenomenon whether it occurs in the old Communist societies or the public sectors of the west. The results certainly have a strong family likeness. If the bulk of American or British economic activity were conducted on the same basis as our education, our societies would be as poor as the old Communist ones.

6 Almost no one today doubts that there are low standards of education in America and Britain. The performance of the weakest students is especially shocking. Vouchers are one way of making schools more responsive to consumer demand. See Arthur Seldon *The Riddle of the Voucher: An Inquiry into the Obstacles to Introducing Choice and Competition in State Schools*. Institute of Economic Affairs, 1986. See also Myron Lieberman *Privatisation and Educational Choice*. Saint Martin's Press, 1989, especially Chapter 5 'Educational Choice as a Means to Educational Improvement'; Alfred O. Hirschman 'Exit and Voice: An Expanding Sphere of Influence' in *Rival Views of Market Society and Other Recent Essays*. Viking, 1987; Antony Flew *Power to the Parents: Reversing Educational Decline*. Sherwood, 1987, pp. 93–111.

7 Charles Murray *Losing Ground: American Social Policy, 1950–1980*. Basic Books, 1984; Charles Murray *The Underclass: The Crisis Deepens*. Institute of Economic Affairs, 1994.

the public choice theorists have shown how the public sector corrupts its workforce. The manifest purpose of the state sector is to provide the public with services. The latent function is self-seeking among its employees.[8]

If public finance means low cognitive standards in school, welfare dependency and subversion of services for private gain, it would seem likely to have implications for intellectual integrity. It would be odd if intellectual life were unscathed by public money, so many other of the latter's unhappy results being widely recognised. True, scholars disagree on what counts as intellectual rigour and decency and therefore on what counts as extremism or corruption. But then there are also those who defend state welfare, saying there is no underclass, no demoralised dependency.[9] In the case of welfare, the fierce defence of an entrenched interest and failed policy has decidedly not prevented the emergence of cases for the prosecution. There has been a genuine for-and-against debate on the welfare consequences of public finance. Nor has loyalty to state production prevented the emergence of public choice theory. A comparable debate is needed on what public finance does to intellectual life, in terms of objectivity, truth and clarity.

Doubtless the state's intellectual employees will proclaim the benefits of public funding till their activities are privatised. Then, most will adapt to the rigours of private finance.[10] Meanwhile, it is fitting that the last unrecognised sin of public sector activity in free societies – its promotion of ideological corruption – should come under full scrutiny. Interested parties will deny or justify the ideological distortion itself. This is not the place

---

8 E. G. West op. cit.

9 Sheldon Danziger 'Overview' in Special Issue, 'Defining and Measuring the Underclass', Focus 12(1), Spring/summer 1989, Institute for Research on Poverty, University of Wisconsin, Madison.

10 It may well prove a case of needs must. The neo-Marxists have certainly felt a sense of loss at the fall of their paradigm. Sometimes the change in their preoccupations is shameful. The first well-known book – effectively a Communist tract – by Samuel Bowles and Herbert Gintis Schooling in Capitalist America. Routledge and Kegan Paul, 1976, was followed a decade later by one which airily dumped their earlier theoretical framework and took up a very sentimental **rightsology**. See their Democracy and Capitalism: Property, Community and the Contradictions of Modernity, Routledge and Kegan Paul, 1986.

to rerun the argument. I take it that Richard Bernstein[11] and Robert Hughes[12] are right about PC in America and Melanie Phillips justified in the British case.[13]

A sustained examination of the links between extremist ideology and public funds is called for, mixing insights from free market reasoning and public choice theory. Effectively, though no one has yet put it thus, this would be to revitalise the sociology of knowledge.[14] This book makes an initial attempt at this, seeking to connect public funds and the emergence of the implacable, endlessly mutating socialist ideologies of western academia.

Markets, knowledge and ideology: the missing links

That the case has not been made before does not mean economists have had nothing to say about questions of knowledge. For example, the case for the superior efficiency of markets holds that no public body could command the information necessary to co-ordinate an economy because that information is immense, unstable and scattered, and no one has the whole picture of varying preferences and relative scarcities. In fact, markets do not 'know' the whole picture either. Markets are not single, conscious minds but aggregations of separate individual intelligences. It is precisely their dispersed character, however, which

---

11 Richard Bernstein *Dictatorship of Virtue*. Knopf, 1994.
12 Robert Hughes *Culture of Complaint*. Harvill, 1994, Lecture 2, 'Multiculti and its Discontents'.
13 Melanie Phillips 'Illiberal Liberalism' in Sarah Dunant (ed.) *The War of the Words*. Virago Press, 1994.
14 Public choice is about the activities of workers in non-market institutions. Sociology of knowledge is about how structures affect intellectual and mental life. The reconcilability of the two seems obvious. Sadly the sociology of knowledge has mostly come to be associated with rather bad theorising about the effects of capitalism and the arbitrariness of intellectual hierarchies. The most influential work in the British case was the reader edited by M. F. D. Young *Knowledge and Control*. Collier Macmillan, 1971. None of the articles in this book defined what was meant by the word 'knowledge', a shortcoming which was to characterise virtually all the literature in this afflatus. The neo-Marxists spent years doing something rather futile. They claimed that a public service activity, education, was fundamentally engaged in the reproduction of the capitalist order. Now if the public choice theorists are right, it is far more plausible to think that institutions run by socialist intellectuals will seek to reproduce socialist ideas and themes and socialist interests. See Dennis O'Keeffe 'The Name of the Game is Weber', *Education Today* 36(2), 1986.

permits much of the picture to be known in bits and pieces. Thus the case is sometimes explicitly reformulated in **epistemic** terms, in the claim that the market economy is a *better knowledge system* than the socialist economy, co-ordinating the available knowledge far more efficiently and comprehensively than any government agency could achieve. This is Hayek's famous argument.[15] Mises argued long ago that socialism was impossible because a planned economy could not identify and co-ordinate the requisite economic data.[16] The point which matters for the privatisation of education, however, is that markets are more resistant than bureaucratic planners to special pleading or vested ideological interests, and that consumer power prevents warping of the curriculum by suppliers' preferences.

Neither have pro-market scholars been blind to the links between intellectual freedom (and political liberty) and markets. Hayek and Mises (and Friedman and the Chicago school) also associate intellectual and political freedom with capitalism.[17] This debate, however, has mostly fixed on whole societies, capitalist or Communist. This is reasonable given our century; but it has left our public sectors rather out of the account in this one

---

15 Friedrich von Hayek 'Economics and Knowledge' in his collection *Individualism and Economic Order* Routledge, 1948. The theme is hugely resisted by educational establishments. They insist, *parti pris*, without decent theoretical cause, that the state must control education, that the experts must plan the curriculum. For an analysis of the planning problem, see also, Friedrich von Hayek 'The Use of Knowledge in Society', *American Economic Review* XXXV(4), September 1945, pp. 519–530. If we translated this brilliant essay into curricular terms, it would argue that the curriculum, like any other activity involving scarcity and choice, is bound to be 'planned'. The question is whether the planning should be:
(1) undertaken on a decentralised basis by the citizens or
(2) concentrated in a centralised bureaucracy, or
(3) in an intermediate solution, entrusted to various near-monopolies.
In the real world there are bound to be elements of (1). In the British case, however, the development of the National Curriculum involves in the main a move from (1) and (3) to (2). The move is away from individual economic agents or large monopolistic examination boards and local inspectorates towards centralised enforcement and a centralised curriculum.
16 Ludwig von Mises *Socialism*. Jonathan Cape, 1936.
17 Friedrich von Hayek *The Road to Serfdom*. Routledge and Kegan Paul, 1944; Mises *op. cit.*; Friedman *op. cit.* These authors just assume that the rule of a socialist bureaucracy would be despotic. All the macro evidence shows this is right. What we must talk about is smaller-scale evidence, the **sectoral** case.

crucial regard. For Hayek, Mises and Friedman *any generally socialist society will be generally unfree*. The further question is rarely if ever put: *in a free society, with a mostly efficient economy, will 'socialist' (publicly financed) enclaves, for example in education, cause pockets of political and cognitive distortion at all comparable to the ills – entrenched onesidedness and error, widespread intellectual persecution and vindictive intolerance – which full socialism entails?*

This book proposes the simple process of going the last mile with what we know already. The public sectors of free societies have been much debated. We know about illiteracy, innumeracy and lack of general knowledge.[18] They *have* been linked with lack of competition and exit.[19] There is also an extensive (non-economic) literature on the ideological excesses of our educational life, including the voluminous debate on PC.[20] This last has *not* often been linked with lack of competition and exit. The Austrians have shown the epistemic deficits of general socialism but have not extended their analysis to ideological questions. Nor has public choice theory dealt with ideological questions significantly. These successful bodies of thought have not advanced the study of socialist ideology under **sectoral socialism.** Why not? Why are there these gaps in the picture?

On the broad front they may reflect the relatively *delayed* role economics has played in the overall analysis of totalitarianism and allied phenomena. Despite the great fame and long-run influence of Hayek's *The Road to Serfdom*,[21] the best-known work defending open societies as morally and politically superior to closed systems like Communism, and as less liable to mental

---

18 Allan Bloom *The Closing of the American Mind*. Simon and Schuster, 1988; Bruce Cooper and Dennis O'Keeffe 'Sweetness and Light in Schools: The Sentimentalisation of Children' in Digby Anderson and Peter Mullen (eds.) *Faking It: The Sentimentalisation of Modern Society*. Penguin, 1998; E. D. Hirsch *Cultural Literacy: What Every American Needs to Know*. Vintage Books, 1988; John Marks *An Anatomy of Failure: Standards in English Schools for 1997*. Social Market Foundation Memorandum, September 1998
19 Seldon *The Riddle of the Voucher op. cit.* See Note 6 above.
20 Accounts hostile to PC include Bernstein *op. cit.*; Hughes *op. cit.*; Phillips *op. cit.*
21 Friedrich von Hayek *The Road to Serfdom op. cit.* This famous book so offended orthodoxies of the time that it had a rather slow start.

distortion, has not usually much stressed the part markets play in this superiority.[22]

Communist economies worked badly – that was taken for granted. Many economists knew why and said so. But the core debate about the totalitarian threat was taken up with the – all too real – evils of Marxist ideology and Communist government, as well as the shorter-lived horrors of Nazism, and the more minor case of Fascism. Certainly the thesis that the conflict was also about markets was much less well known. Indeed, the economic theorists best placed to celebrate the market were for decades not given pre-eminence even on their home ground, much less in the struggle against totalitarianism. The seminal market theorising of the Austrian and Chicago schools[23] was long regarded as somewhat marginal by mainstream economists even *vis-à-vis* market economies, let alone socialist ones, at a time when non-economist critics of Communism, such as Orwell, Koestler and Silone, were already household names.[24] Popper was well read in economics; but even he was not an economist.

---

22 Arthur Koestler's *Darkness at Noon* and George Orwell's *1984* are obvious examples; but more academic studies conform to the same pattern. Karl Popper's *The Open Society and its Enemies*. Routledge, 1962 is a case in point.

23 By these seminal theorists I mean Hayek and Friedman and their colleagues. They had for decades to fight the entrenched Keynesianism of academic and government establishments. Then there were quasi-socialist economists like Galbraith. It seems unlikely that Galbraith's reputation will survive as well as Hayek's or Friedman's will; but he reached a much wider audience than they for a long time. It is scarcely surprising then, that their critiques of socialism did not reach the same width of audience initially as *Darkness at Noon* or *1984* or Ignazio Silone's *Fontamara*.

24 It is a fair generalisation that in the 30 years following the Second World War, the novelists (Orwell and Koestler) and the social theorists (Popper and Aron) were more influential against Communism than were the economists. Even now Orwell and Koestler, for all their brilliance quite deficient in economic understanding, remain the most famous critics of totalitarian socialism. *1984* and *Darkness at Noon* were far more important in the battle against Communism than *The Road to Serfdom*. George Orwell, who wrote a half-hearted review of *The Road to Serfdom* (in an untitled review in the *Observer*, 9 April 1944 where among other adverse remarks we find: 'The trouble with competitions is that somebody loses them'; see Sonia Orwell and Ian Angus (eds) *Orwell, The Collected Essays* etc., Vol. 3, 'As I Please'. Penguin, 1968. pp. 142–144) had still not struggled out of his socialist straitjacket at the time of his death in 1950, and Koestler never really got to grips with the political economy of capitalism. All this is to be regretted. Had the market economists carried the day sooner, Communism might well have fallen sooner.

Certainly economic theory was in no sense central to his anti-totalitarian writings.[25]

Today, scholars increasingly recognise that crucial sub-systems in free societies, notably education and welfare, belong to the socialist genus. A leading American spokesman for a teachers' union has said the same. The late Albert Shanker, former president of the American Federation of Teachers, has said that American education 'operates like a planned economy... it's no surprise our school system doesn't improve ... it ... resembles the Communist economy'.[26]

Yet even now the falsity and bias of much of the western intelligentsia has not been much related to that absence or attenuation of markets which sectoral socialism entails. The public finance background of ideological excess has not been much probed.[27] Indeed, leading political theorists John Gray and Norman Barry have assured me there is no such relationship.[28] They are talking, one notes, of public finance and socialist radicalism in free societies. If they were looking at general socialism, they could hardly fail to spot the links.

Russia, China, Cuba, etc. have been cases in point, without nuance, full-blooded examples of socialism, whose moral and intellectual bankruptcy matches and intertwines with their economic failure. The case before us *is* nuanced: the effects on scholarly integrity of state-financed education in non-socialist societies. What are the likely effects on educational decision-making, both on the demand and supply side, of the subsidisation by the tax-payer of the decisions in question?

Intellectual distortion counterfactually considered

Rich modern societies have elaborate education systems, inevitably, given their specialised division of intellectual labour.

---

25 Popper *op. cit.* This book contains little by way of defence of the free market.

26 Albert Shanker quoted in Ken Gannicott *Taking Education Seriously: A Reform Program for Australia's Schools*. The Centre for Independent Studies, 1997, p. 16. Taken from the *Wall Street Journal,* 2 October 1989, quoted in turn from A. Shanker 'Where We Stand', *New Republic,* 4 November 1986.

27 I have previously linked it not so much with private finance as with the growth of the state, which may come to much the same thing. See Dennis J. O'Keeffe *The Wayward Elite.* Adam Smith Institute, 1990. For the beginnings of an impressive formal analysis see David Frum 'It's Big Government Stupid' in *Commentary* June 1994.

28 I refer not to published controversy but to repeated private exchanges.

The wrong turns in modern education resemble those leading to other versions of economic inefficiency. Suppliers devise a curriculum and pedagogy incorporating their preferences, and are not brought to financial account for policy failures. Similarly, choice of subject-matter by students is not hard-headed realism; it is a subsidised choice. It seems unlikely, for example, that the enormous expansion of social science in America and Britain in the last 40 years, could have happened on a market basis. It was a tax-based curricular consumption spree.

Intellectual integrity is an analogue of epistemic accuracy. People will be truer to the severe canons when their own resources are on the line. The ideological subversion lurking within public spending is one more aspect of the latter's economic inefficiency. Many of the attitudes of the educational élite virtually guarantee the misuse of resources and pave the way for more exotic extremism. Some of their views are truly odd in the wider context of successful market economies. The hatred of competition and meritocracy, the scorn for public opinion, the extreme defensiveness about standards, the reflex repudiation of all criticism: these are not the attitudes which created the astonishing wealth and freedoms of modernity. It should seem extraordinary to all and sundry that these Caliban postures and evasions should be prime values in the educational institutions of the richest societies in history. That it does not astonish us shows the power of habituation. In living memory many schools and colleges have lost their guardianship character, their reasonable small 'c' conservatism in curriculum and teaching, their automatic consistency with what is routinely understood as decent. They have become all too often mediocre and at their worst even agencies of disruption.

Our intellectual life, our curriculum and methods of teaching are not static – they would have changed in some degree had education not been absorbed by the state. They would have remained anchored, however, in the ideas and attitudes which have underpinned the growth of our civilisation from the nineteenth century. In the event, long exposure to improperly audited public finance has eventually wrenched them all to some degree away from the traditions of rigour, tolerance and decency which Western societies inherited from the ancient civilisation of Europe and from the Enlightenment. A free market in education would have protected these traditions. Public finance has led to their partial erosion.

The intellectual disfiguration of the academy in such societies as ours is a commonplace.[29] The way propaganda is often presented in schools and universities as proper sociology or social administration is now well charted. David Marsland in Britain[30] and Irving Horowitz in the USA[31] have made it clear that these subjects are typically vitiated by egalitarian obsessions. Humanities teaching too has often been discredited by antinomian bias.[32] As for teacher education, its distortions have been logged both in Britain[33] and in America.[34]

This book, then, fixes only on the underinvestigated links between well-known phenomena. The neglect of these links is one of the strangest in modern social science. The argument needs, however, a strong caveat: intellectual corruption is not to be *mechanistically* associated with public finance. In the free societies those occasions when public finance is properly employed may well exceed those when it is abused, though in the educational and welfare cases the incidence of abuse has increased dramatically in recent decades. Moreover, markets too can register perverse choices. Private finance can pursue inane or even insane causes. Indeed, since Utopia, as the name suggests, is unattainable, extremism will be with us always in some degree. There will always be corruption, including intellectual corruption, in society. It will happen in market economies too. The point, however, is that it is much more typical of the socialist organisation of resources, especially as constrained by the ideologies which also drive socialism. The problem of corruption is to attenuate it. This, it seems to me, requires our breaking free of the present publicly financed educational straitjacket which hinders the free societies.

The appeal of private finance is, to speak analogously, neo-Darwinian, in that it will tend to block that which is unpopular

29 For a brilliant account of the obscurantism affecting the humanities and social science see Christopher Lasch *The Revolt of the Elites*. Norton, 1994, Chapter 10, 'Academic Pseudo-radicalism'.
30 David Marsland *Seeds of Bankruptcy*. Claridge, 1988.
31 Irving Louis Horowitz 'The Decomposition of Sociology', *Academic Questions,* Spring 1992.
32 Lasch *op. cit.*; Bloom *op. cit.*; Hughes *op. cit.*
33 O'Keeffe *The Wayward Elite op. cit.*
34 Rita Kramer *Ed School Follies: The Miseducation of America's Teachers*. Free Press, 1991.

or repugnant to common sense, that is to say not consistent with the pyschological and moral environment, and also tend over time to winnow out that which is illogical or inconsistent with the evidence, that is to say does not accord with the epistemic environment. As our century has shown, error and absurdity are most vulnerable in open societies, or, putting the case the other way round, flourish best in the ambience of closed and explicit ideologies like those in the totalitarian societies.

Accordingly, my argument follows a counterfactual line, criticising present arrangements from the standpoint of what might have been or might yet be. Arthur Seldon's reader has set a recent precedent here, exploring in the British instance what might have been very different histories of education, health, insurance, charity and so on, had the state not so comprehensively intervened.[35] The crux of the matter as it concerns PC and related extremism, is the claim that the present level of agitation *vis-à-vis* race, sex, multiculture, etc. could not have built up without public funds. There would not have been sufficient private demand.

This proposition merely takes a generally established thesis – that socialism is a corrupt form of human governance – and develops a sub-thesis from it. We know that general socialism (Communism) is always disastrous, and we know that a partially socialised society can be equally so if the civil order is suppressed (as in Nazism). This book merely tries to show that socialist educational arrangements can generate substantial ideological discord even when the economy remains overwhelmingly a market-based one and when the civil order is still strong. The public sectors of free societies – among many adverse achievements – have been very successful in generating socialist ideologies.

Artefacts of public money in the absence of markets

Socialist ideology in its various forms, including PC, is an artefact of public money, just as welfare dependency is. Indeed, the critique of ideological excess is actually part of the wider critique of the welfare state. To avoid corruption, ideas, like individuals, should generally make their own way financially.

---

35 Arthur Seldon (ed.) *Reprivatising Welfare After the Lost Century op. cit.*

26

To understand PC and kindred phenomena, we must understand the mental life of the public sector, i.e. of socialism itelf. This calls for a revivified sociology of knowledge, one stripped of its habitual but now redundant Marxist baggage. The sociology of knowledge explains ideas in terms of the social structures in which they flourish. We may expect low standards and ideological waywardness from socialist education in free societies, in the same way and for the same reasons we have learned to expect them from generally socialist societies.

The typical economic mode of American and British education is given by:

- public finance

- suppression of competition

- suppression of the rational division of labour

- demonetised transactions

- moral hazard

- fiscal illusion

- ruthless jockeying of élite groups for rent and position.

These are the conditions of socialist demarketisation. The first four are specifics of the Marxist vision and the latter three observable empirical conditions of the excising of capitalist logic from production. Moral hazard refers to the coarsening of moral life which often happens when people's choices are not exercised via their own resources. The normal risks of market decisions are much reduced. Public sector bureaucrats or welfare dependants spend other people's incomes (or rather portions of incomes taken from people via taxation). Such bureaucrats and dependants are morally at risk precisely because their own personal financial risk is removed or much lessened.

At the same time the remoteness of production from payment, via the tax mechanism, produces the illusion among citizens that it is costless. This encourages frivolous, irresponsible consumption. Finally, power is remorselessly concentrated on the supply side of production, though this may not mean that the initiative lies solely or even mainly with those doing the teaching. In fact in America and Britain alike there is a struggle for power going on between teachers and bureaucrats, one which the bureaucrats seem to be winning.[36]

Whichever group predominates, the suppliers of educational services at university level are likely to be fortified by compulsory education at the primary and secondary stages. In a formal pre-university exposure lasting, say, 13 years, the fact that for most or even all of them the students must attend, has implications for the whole experience. The suppliers of education in its compulsory stage are likely to share the convictions of tertiary suppliers, especially those in teacher education. The managerial élite by definition have an overwhelming ascendancy as to what gets supplied. Such compulsion has not been much analysed. There may be very good reasons for it; but *a priori* reflection suggests that it represents a huge intrusion into family life by the state and by definition a weakening of the curricular discretion of the public.

These ill effects could be more than compensated if compulsory attendance strengthened the civil order or economic life. We do not know how far our educational arrangements remain beneficial overall. We must also assume that compulsory education enjoys wide public endorsement in our two countries. This does not mean that a supply-led curriculum and pedagogy are appropriate to a free society. The demand for private schooling is growing in America. In the British case polling might well show overwhelming support for compulsion; but there is a

---

36 In Britain the centralisation of universities in general and teacher education in particular has gone hand in hand with the development of the National Curriculum for schools. In the late 1980s, when the Russians were telling the world that bureaucratic centralism is a hopeless way of organising anything, the British started imposing it on their education system. In America, since Chubb and Moe first announced that the fundamental educational problem was stifling bureaucracy, (see John E. Chubb and Terry M. Moe *Politics, Markets and America's Schools,* Brookings Institution, 1990) there has been repeated advocacy of greater choice. There seems little evidence that this has happened. Bureaucracy confines teachers as much as students. To get anywhere near market optimality in curriculum we need free teachers confronting free citizens in a free market. Tony Green, reviewing the Chubb and Moe book far from negatively, says we have never tried out a full market in education, so we do not know what would result. (Anthony Green in *British Journal of Sociology of Education* 12(3), 1991, p. 390.) Green here implies that education is different from other goods. As always with this claim, we are not told how. And we know the general case. Markets work, socialism does not and bureaucracy makes everything worse.

growing repugnance for handing production over to the state. More and more citizens say they would pay privately if they could afford it.[37] Most citizens would not put it in sophisticated terms. Perhaps, though, they *do* think education does not sustain the civil order or market economy adequately. The desire for private schooling does suggest that demand needs resensitising and reinvigorating.

The fatal embrace: the state and socialist ideas

Neo-Marxist education theory made capitalism problematic and counterfactually linked its survival to the functions of the education system. School was said to 'endorse' capitalism, a proposition wildly remote from any decent evidence.[38] A far more convincing project would be the counterfactual rethinking of our modern educational history along market-oriented lines. It is the public sector which should be seen as problematic, given its appalling track record. A revived sociology of knowledge would aid our understanding of the impact of public money on the organisation of knowledge and ideology. Although free enterprise is to be associated with epistemic accuracy, socialist education, like all socialism, is liable to producer-capture and tendentious distortion. Though it was Marxism which promoted the sociology of knowledge, there is no intrinsic reason this branch of sociology should have a pro-socialistic bias, a point even Karl Popper seems to have gone wrong on.[39] Markets are social phenomena tending to accuracy in their search for information. It is socialist production which is more obviously subject to ideological distortion.[40]

It has already been conceded, however, that there is no mechanistic link between public finance and such distortion.

---

37 *Attitudes to Independent Schools* MORI (for the Independent Schools Information Service), October 1998.
38 There is a truly vast literature here. See as very typical Bowles and Gintis *Schooling in Capitalist America op. cit.*. Our educational arrangements involve socialist *and* market influences. The whole neo-Marxist project of interpreting them almost entirely on pro-capitalist lines was intrinsically flawed. Why should a public sector agency, run by socialists (US 'liberals') on a largely monopolistic basis, with an ever growing 'egalitarian' agenda which in its latest form has coalesced into PC, be thought as fundamentally committed to capitalist imperatives?
39 Popper *op. cit.* Vol 2, Chapter 23.
40 O'Keeffe 'The Name of the Game is Weber' *op. cit.*

This is not surprising; indeed it is typical of the relationships social science uncovers. The preliminary evidence which opponents of my thesis might appeal to is clear enough. In America there are private universities which are PC and state ones which are not.[41] Moreover, in the USA private universities made the early running for PC, backed up by the big private foundations.[42] It is also the case that at primary and secondary levels of education the ideas – child-centred education, etc. – which seem to have been most destructive, were evolved and tried out in private schools initially. Indeed, socialist theory as we now know it has its modern origins in private research and reflection often predating and mostly independent of public education systems until the late nineteenth century.[43]

All this is true. To accede to it, however, is to admit rather little. Marx lived a life of dependency and sponging in a capitalist society.[44] That does not make markets and the free civil order responsible for Communism. The issue is: what *arrangements* realise the evils scholars dream up, wherever they happen to dream them? All totalitarian systems require a vast expansion of the state, far beyond the limits of a free society. Nazi and Fascist economic life involved an expansive growth in fiscal socialism, that is socialism based on government tax revenues rather than actual state production.[45] The more ambitious Communist version entailed society-wide attempts at directly managed production as well as near universal public finance, attempts which have now collapsed almost everywhere leaving a legacy of horror and farce in their wake.

By definition, socialist education in the free societies, though a vast undertaking, is dwarfed by these totalitarian experiments. Education in free societies cannot produce society-wide

---

41 Some of the most prestigious private universities are deeply affected by PC, whereas George Mason, a state university, is home to the spirit of the market and to traditional small 'c' conservative values.

42 Chester E. Finn Jr 'Giving it Away', *Salisbury Review* Summer 1998, pp. 15–19.

43 Much of the socialist tradition was under way before compulsory education became a reality in Britain or America.

44 Leopold Schwarzschild *The Red Prussian*. Pickwick Books, 1986.

45 Harold James *The German Slump: Politics and Economics, 1924–1936*. Clarendon Press, 1986, Chapter IX. Oddly James denies that it was socialism but his account makes it clear that this is what it was.

socialism. Nor can it achieve evil on anything remotely like the scale of full socialism. Nor, indeed, do its managers try to. It does, nevertheless, reproduce some comparable trends in miniature. To begin with, the finance of our education is inherently chaotic. Most of our educational expenditures involve party A being taxed by party B so that party C can employ party D to teach party E. This exemplifies the worst kind of circuitous finance, where the persons taxed are hopelessly remote from the people the funds are used on. Bruce Cooper and Sheree Speakman remind us of the further related fault, that most of the funds are siphoned off en route.[46] The question not directly asked by Cooper and Speakman is the one which bothers me: just what do all the funds finance, whether they get to the classroom or not?

Risk, resource use and public finance

In a seminal essay, David Frum has argued that public finance changes the *pattern of risk* and therefore of the use of resources.[47] This has effects on personnel and output. The standard criticism of public finance merely argues that if you replace private by public finance in an activity you either get a fall in output for the same factor-input, or you must increase the factor input. In fact, Frum observes, when you change the pattern of risk you get *different outputs*. This is an extremely fertile insight which the supporters of freedom should pursue vigorously until it is absorbed as a commonplace. In the case of education, for example, I suggest, public finance does not just mean inefficiency, the same curriculum costing more or shrinking – it means a different curriculum. It means different teaching, different examinations. It means a whole new range of personnel. The conditions and composition of American and British intellectual activity have been profoundly modified for the worse by the introduction and hypertrophy of socialist education in our two societies.

Capitalism thrives on advantageous discovery and innovation. Its entrepreneurs are always at risk, however. Discovery

---

46 Cooper and Speakman are talking about the finance of American schools. In principle most public finance must be subject to this question of frictional loss. See Bruce Cooper and Sheree T. Speakman *Optimizing Educational Resources*. JAI Press, 1996, especially Chapter 7 'Tracing School Site Expenditure: Equity, Policy and Legal Implications'.

47 Frum *op. cit.*

and innovation are not extinguished in the public sectors of the free societies, but they are *greatly distorted by public finance*. Costs are heavily socialised and benefits to innovators much enhanced by the reduction of risk which public finance effects. Once entrepreneurship is effectively debased in this way, once innovation is not punished for failure, unrepresentative material soon gets bedded in and the curriculum becomes increasingly remote from standard preferences and preoccupations.

Chapter 2 will seek to characterise PC and related thought more fully. Chapter 3 will examine in detail the predominantly socialist nature of our educational and intellectual life in countries like America and Britain, 'socialism' meaning the union of egalitarian ideology and public finance. Chapter 4 explores in counterfactual vein the political economy of intellectual life in free societies which have socialist educational arrangements, seeking to pin down as tightly as possible the role of public finance in our intellectual woes. The analysis seeks to uncover in what ways such intellectual life might have evolved differently had it been entrusted to private finance. Finally, Chapter 5 continues the counterfactual theme, proposing that the intellectual reversal of socialism in our educational arrangements demands its material reversal too. It calls accordingly for the radical privatisation of our educational institutions.

2 | The what and the where of PC

Introduction

Socialism is a mix of ideas and institutions. The main *theme* of socialist ideology is equality; the main *scheme* of socialist institutions is public finance. PC is the latest, most extreme socialist ideology, in overall terms inconceivable without the sustaining support of the taxpayer. Admittedly, PC now occurs in many non-socialist contexts. Why should it not? It is a colonising infection which has spread. The private sector of the economy and the civil order of society are not immune to public sector diseases. Indeed, awareness that this is so is one factor driving the writing of this monograph.

PC subsumes all the equality obsessions. At its core, however, we find the familiar trio: race, sex and culture. These core cults have all failed to retain their egalitarian postures in their original form, a point which will be very important when we try to classify PC politically. Today the campaigns which once preached universal equality have splintered. Some of their exponents now assert the *inferiority* of whites, men and European culture. Nevertheless the original mantras remain familiar. The sexes are equal, as are all races and cultures. Any inequalities between them are unjust and must be removed.

Like so many misleading ideas, these egalitarian campaigns began in true perceptions. Racial and sexual hatred and cultural intolerance *are* destructive and philistine. Sadly, modern campaigns against them have bit by bit lost their reasonableness and sobriety. They were soon recast in new, extreme and threatening terms. The best indicator of this is not anything empirically charted – though a vast range of examples is available – but what anyone can pick up in the atmosphere of certain parts of modern America and Britain: the fanaticism, nervousness, spite and embarrassment which so often surround sexual, racial and cultural relations. There is a disposition amongst intellectuals in the richest and securest societies in history to find oppressions

33

all around, and in particular a propensity amongst middle-class white men to offer cringing apologies for alleged crimes in the past associated with their sex, race and cultural characteristics.

Some of the crimes are real, but an air of unreality surrounds their recitation. No whites in America or Britain are guilty today of enslaving others, any more than any men are guilty of the injustice done to women by nineteenth-century property laws. The roots of this kind of guilty misconception are undoubtedly old; but its modern expression appears to be a function more than anything else of soft, easy public funds which no one audits properly. And few people seem to dare tell the truth: America and Britain are *fortunate places to be for almost all those who live in them.* The case to the contrary is mostly publicly financed mischief.

PC is a socialist phenomenon

Sometimes socialist intentions are advisedly confessed by the protagonists of various PC persuasions. The militant feminist Alison Jaggar, in a sinister argument proposing that science commit itself to devising ways for men to produce babies' milk and women to fertilise each other, speaks of 'the ultimate transformation of human nature at which *socialist* feminists aim'[48] [my italics].

Unfortunately Jaggar's aggression is not unusual. The **separatism** of her ideas is obvious even in a short extract. The socialism in question, it seems, is to be reserved for women. Today, former egalitarian claims *vis-à-vis* race, the sexes and cultures have now all been rivalled by new claims for *inequality*. Some feminists believe women must be equal among themselves, but that women as a sex are superior, certain black intellectuals preach the egalitarian solidarity of African race and culture but also their relative superiority, and multiculturalism has passed from arguing that non-western cultures are as good as western culture to the claim that the latter is an enemy oppressing the former.[49] These developments involve a reversion from universal

---

48 Alison Jaggar *Feminist Politics and Human Nature.* Rowman and Allanheld, 1983, p. 132.
49 Robert Hughes *op. cit.* Lecture 2 'Multi Culti and its Discontents'; Steven Yates *Civil Wrongs: What Went Wrong With Affirmative Action.* Institute for Contemporary Studies Press, 1994, Chapter 3.

humanism to **particularist** separatism, the reassertion of **ascriptive** reasoning, a reborn fatalism in our affairs. PC and radical egalitarianism are thus strung out between contradictory or rival claims and counterclaims. Vice in particular is differentially distributed, it would seem. 'All whites are racist ... and only whites are racist.' 'All men are sexist.' In recent decades these slogans have been commonplace.

PC's roots in the child-centred revolution

Militant egalitarianism is both incoherent and unstable. It is also destabilising in its effects. But the origins and affinities of PC are not always fully appreciated. The question is not just what its discernible modern 'building block' components are, but what *steps* in our educational and social thought have led up to it. Further back in time lie pointers – like PC today these were overwhelmingly in public sector education – in the same direction, like the oft-heard claim that 'we teach children not subjects', a modern version of Rousseau's romanticism, which effectively holds that childhood is as important as adulthood, i.e. that children and adults are 'equal'.[50] Once this view has been accepted the antinomian flood is already in a position to pour through open gates.

Perhaps those who dismantled adult authority did not know what they were doing. Or perhaps they did. Tradition said children go to school to learn to be adults eventually, not to have their childhood confirmed indefinitely. Now that child–adult equality is institutionalised, however, the once outlandish view has become acceptable and widely accepted.

The campaigns which stressed spontaneity in writing of English against formal accomplishment in spelling, syntax and grammar[51] and which ousted traditional mastery of preliminary mathematical rote learning, were extensions of this childhood equality theme.[52] Adults must not oppress children by violating

---

50 Dennis O'Keeffe 'Diligence Abandoned' in Digby Anderson (ed.) *The Loss of Virtue*. Social Affairs Unit, 1992.
51 Alan Barcan 'English: Two Decades of Attrition' in Dennis O'Keeffe (ed.) *The Wayward Curriculum*. Social Affairs Unit, 1986.
52 Colin Coldman and Ken Shepherd 'Mathematics: The Campaign for 'Real Maths' in Secondary Schools' in O'Keeffe *The Wayward Curriculum*.

their right to an unharassed childhood.[53] No one in the movements which have in considerable degree infantilised our populations had PC in mind. But root incompetence, factual ignorance and widespread relativism *are* today's problems at university as Allan Bloom observed,[54] and they go back to earlier school errors in the egalitarian ascendancy. They are necessary conditions of PC and other 'antischolarship' as Yates calls it.[55]

Related pathologies

PC is very close to multiculturalism, the doctrine that all cultures must be considered equal, all equally relative to the contexts which produced them, none possessing greater authority than any other.[56] In its turn multiculturalism is very like relativism. Relativism has been the most successful form of modern **nihilism**. It treats mental life as always and only a function of the particular power structures of time and place, such that there are no transcultural objective truths.[57] Such are PC's main – and unstable – ideological co-ordinates.

Daniel Johnson has represented PC as the *penultimate* stage of western self-destruction. The ultimate version for him, 'blatant' in America, 'latent' in Britain, is the new cultural assault, the war against the western artistic canon, an assault which he says goes beyond PC.[58]

In fact it does not. PC subsumes precisely an 'egalitarian' critique of high culture. It is an easy step from arguing that

---

53 For a good discussion of the child-centred view see E. D. Hirsch Jr *The Schools We Need and Why We Don't Have Them*. Doubleday, 1996, especially Chapters 3 and 4.

54 Bloom *op. cit.*

55 Yates *op. cit.*

56 Robert Hughes is one of a number of writers who understand multiculturalism in a favourable sense, one entailing openness and the absence of cultural bigotry. See Hughes *op. cit.* Hughes is, however, deeply hostile to PC. On the whole I have found that 'multiculturalism' is best understood pejoratively by those who favour the free society. See for example, Bernstein *op. cit.*; Dennis O'Keeffe 'Multiculturalism and Cultural Literacy' in Geoff Partington (ed.) *Cultural Literacy, International Journal of Social Education* 9(1), Spring/Summer 1994; John O'Sullivan 'The Next Great Threat to Liberal Democracy', *Daily Telegraph*, 8 March 1999.

57 For a critique see Roger Scruton *Modern Philosophy*. Sinclair Stevenson, 1994.

58 Daniel Johnson 'Enter the New Nihilists', *The Daily Telegraph*, November 7, 1998, p. 24.

this or that product is 'equal' to Shakespeare to claiming that the mere existence of the Shakespearean corpus is oppressive. For decades it has been possible to read for a degree in English in some universities, both in the USA and in Britain, without studying Shakespeare, Chaucer or Milton. Virtually all undergraduates in English now have to read 'theory' courses, however, which are largely PC. Johnson was moved to write following the hostility to Shakespeare recently witnessed at Arizona State University.[59] This is no more than an expression of PC impulses in the public curriculum.

PC combines ideologies and practices – what Marxists used to call a '**praxis**'. As a praxis, it closely resembles Affirmative Action and Equal Opportunities; they incorporate the same ideology. Like them it has intimate links with the welfare state in general.[60] In the British case, Leo McKinstry has stressed the PC ideas which underlie much welfare administration, such as hostility to any expression of preference for heterosexual love or traditional married domesticity. The British Labour government 'has shied away from measures that would actually uphold the traditional idea of marriage'.[61]

The PC 'patch'

PC has a large patch it dominates in higher education, particularly in teacher education, arts and social sciences, theoretical and applied. Secondary and even primary schools are sometimes affected, too, especially by sentimental versions of environmentalism.[62] PC is also strong in parts of the media – for TV and cinema the story will tell itself to most viewers – and publishing.[63] Yates claims that in America PC is a major force in private commerce.[64]

---

59 *Ibid.*
60 Yates *op. cit.* especially Chapter 4.
61 Leo McKinstry 'The emptiness of Labour's new policy on marriage'. *Sunday Telegraph*, 1 November 1998, p. 35.
62 Anthony O'Hear *Nonsense about Nature,* Social Affairs Unit, 1997.
63 Many American and British films and TV programmes are PC. There is a heavy bias in publishing too. Geoff Dench's fine book on feminism failed to get a British publisher and he was forced to publish in America where the size of the market affords some protection. See Geoff Dench *Transforming Men: Changing Patterns of Dependency and Dominance in gender Relations,* Transaction, 1996.
64 Yates *op. cit.* Chapter 1. I find Yates's evidence here rather thin.

Robert Halfon makes much the same case for British business.[65] We should not think PC has swept the corporate boardrooms; but it has clearly not been confined to educational barracks. Moreover, as Chester Finn reminds us, PC is very strong in the big American charitable foundations.[66]

These varying contexts have different PC emphases. Primary and secondary schools affected tend to concentrate on the environment and pollution. The more intense campaigns against racism, sexism and Eurocentrism mostly belong to university social science and literature departments and teacher education,[67] though they have influenced primary and secondary schools too, as in America in the case of the 'African American Baseline Essays' from Portland, Oregon.[68] The reproduction of the PC institutional patch is secured by the endless PC exchange between publishing and show business and state education.[69]

PC's codes of practice

PC's 'codes' of practice – mostly informal in both America and Britain – contain numerous protocols governing what people can or cannot say or write or generally do. They cover even such issues as our clothes, the looks we allow on our faces, or even the body language, as human gesture and posture are now called, we present to others.

PC's concerns overlap with the overheated insistence on rights which is current today, as well as with the habit of dividing the world into oppressors/exploiters and their victims.[70] In addition PC has links with the green movement, with New Ageism/Post-Modernism and with the neo-pagan cults which either contend

---

65 Robert Halfon *Corporate Irresponsibility: Is Business Appeasing Anti-Business Activists?* Social Affairs Unit, 1998.

66 Finn *op. cit.* Once funds are accumulated for mischievous purposes, they are part of the wherewithal of fiscal socialism.

67 Kramer *op. cit.*; O'Keeffe *The Wayward Elite op. cit.*

68 Hughes *op. cit.,* pp. 111–112.

69 The education system sets up a direct demand for commercial PC books and supplies an indoctrinated public for PC films and so on.

70 'Rights' are often a misnomer for entitlements of a conventional kind sometimes voluntarily agreed to by taxpayers, often more or less coercively lifted by the state. See Yates *op. cit.,* Chapter 6.

with established religion or seek to subvert it from within. [71] PC's advocates also seem to be pro-abortion and the legitimation of homosexuality, whilst maintaining a hostility to the smoking of tobacco. This last grouping has no binding logic. It is merely a contingent package on the outer fringe of PC.

The overall PC package is neither unitary nor coherent. PC proper often goes with ideas which exist quite independently, supported by people remote from most PC concerns. The present hostility to smoking is an example, as are reasonable versions of concern for the environment and animal welfare. As to coherence, though there is a core PC, contradictions abound even in this core. Indeed, the movement is not a precise thing. Rather it is a motley clutch of ideas united mainly by their hostility to our traditional western ways and arrangements. There is no deep logic in the fact that AIDS is PC and lung cancer not, for example. It is a result of the contingent fact that PC militates in favour of the homosexual minority and against tobacco.

There is no intrinsic reason PC should be hostile to smoking. Since the smoking of tobacco comes from aboriginal peoples in America who were there before the whites arrived, and whose subsequent gross ill-treatment by the whites is not only a historical truth but also a favourite multicultural theme, one might expect smoking to be well regarded by multiculturalism.[72] By the same token multiculturalists, who claim there is no such thing as superior cultures – specifically that western cultures are in no sense superior to non-western – could conceivably be hostile to abortion. It was roundly condemned and punished by many non-European cultures, the Incas, for example.[73]

Rather than pursuing every idea or practice which might belong to the PC mind-set, we should focus on PC's inner core: the modern cults of equality. Their extreme instability – their endlessly mutating character – does not in any way render them less toxic. Their sole abiding feature is a malignant determinism

---

71 For a good discussion of pagan influences on the feminist wing of PC, see Cornelia Ferrera 'Isis and the Crisis of Morality' in Christine M. Kelly (ed.) *The Enemy Within: Radical Feminism in the Christian Churches*. Family Publications, 1992.

72 Smoking might have been endorsed, like pop music, because of the level of working-class participation and enthusiasm.

73 Igor Shafarevich *The Socialist Phenomenon*. Harper and Row, 1990, p. 274.

and collectivism contradictorily combined with a ferocious moralistic denunciation of their enemies.

PC: core concerns and contentions

PC's core concerns can be specified easily: the dynamics of sexual, racial and cultural power. In recent decades sexual, racial and cultural relations in Western societies have been subjected to sustained egalitarian critique.[74] PC and its ideological allies insist that our societies are riddled with prejudices against women, non-whites, minority cultures and homosexuals, and marked by ill-treatment of people in these categories. Our society is held to be an unequal (hierarchical) power structure which reproduces these biases, through oppression, exploitation and other ill-treatment. The wrongs PC opposes are alleged to be the defining ones of our way of life.

No textbooks, no single authority nor even group of authorities represent PC. The attacks made on it are equally diffuse. Robert Hughes's brilliant critique perversely manages not to notice how intertwined PC is with the welfare state in the USA.[75] The late Christopher Lasch even produced a magnificent chapter in one of his last books on precisely the sort of convoluted language and mental atmosphere as well as special interest group pleading which support PC, without actually mentioning the latter by name.[76] All this fuzziness is the less surprising if we note – as we must – that some people believe that PC does not even exist.

Is there such a thing as PC?

Debate continues as to PC's nature and threat, if any. Three main positions are apparent. First that PC is a deplorable reality;[77] second that PC is a justified reality;[78] and third – a

---

74 Hughes *op. cit.*; Yates *op. cit.*; Kramer *op. cit.*; O'Keeffe *The Wayward Elite op. cit.*

75 Hughes *op. cit.* especially Lecture 1.

76 Lasch *op. cit.,* Chapter 10.

77 Roger Kimball *Tenured Radicals.* Harper and Row, 1990; Dinesh D'Souza *Illiberal Education.* Free Press, 1991.

78 Stanley Fish *Professional Correctness: Literary Studies and Political Change.* Clarendon Press, 1995. This is an incoherent book in which Fish's genuine literary learning grinds against his sociological ignorance. He seeks both to justify the politicisation of literature and to persuade us that this is not much of a threat.

rather exotic claim – that PC does not really exist at all, being only a construct or figment of indignant reactionary scholarship.[79]

There are more nuanced versions. Professor Hall sympathises with PC ideas but says they make him nervous.[80] Others say the movement is proper but weak.[81] Yet others have maintained that the movement is odious but much frailer than its enemies have usually painted it.[82]

The best-known work alleging that there is actually no such thing as PC is by John K. Wilson.[83] His book has some initial plausibility. As Roger Scruton has observed, some of the early opponents of PC were careless with their factual accounts and without doubt some of the worst excesses on American campuses were soon 'scotched by conservative antibodies'.[84] Where Wilson's argument fails, however, as Scruton notes, is in its educational understanding. He sees the world in terms of adversarial claims and counterclaims. He has no sense of education being the search for what is true, or beautiful or morally binding. His is the outlook of the socialist ideologue: education is for him a political and ideological struggle for supremacy, waged by opposing interest groups and factions. It is not an intellectual inquiry after truth by a community of scholars, united by a certain consensus on standards of argument and evidence, however much they may disagree.

This disposition to see intellectual life as a battle the big battalions will win, rather than a debate in which one hopes truth will out, this 'might is right' view of the mental world, is the core of relativism and has an ancient pedigree. More locally

---

79 John K. Wilson *The Myth of Political Correctness*. Duke University Press, 1995.
80 Stuart Hall 'Some Politically Incorrect Pathways Through PC' in Sarah Dunant (ed.) *The War of the Words: The Political Correctness Debate*. Virago, 1994.
81 Meera Syall *PC: GLC* in Dunant *op. cit.*
82 This view was put to me by Professor George Kateb of Princeton.
83 Wilson *op. cit.*
84 Roger Scruton 'Opening Fire in the Real Culture Wars', *The Times*, 4 January 1996. In any case see also for an unanswerable empirical charting of PC in American academia Alan Charles Kors and Harvey Silvergate *The Shadow University: The Betrayal of Liberty on America's Campuses*. Free Press, 1998. Nigel Ashford, in a most perceptive review of this text says that the kind of closure – denial of free speech, for example – now obvious in American universities, is probably present in British ones too, though the research has not been done. See 'Reviews' *Free Life*, 29 April 1999, pp. 7–8.

and recently, it is the fruit of decades of Marxisant sociology of knowledge. Popper produced a magisterial critique of this persuasion back in the 1950s.[85] That any so-called scholar could think like Wilson shows just how far the PC view has prevailed. Many university teachers and other nominally educated people in America and Britain see the world in exactly such terms, and this group includes lots who would not accept the label PC, or even reject it indignantly.

PC: some notable contemporary examples

The extent to which PC has penetrated and unsettled the mental life of our societies is frightening. In February 1999 there were some notable examples in America and Britain. A man in Washington was in trouble with the black lobby for using the word 'niggardly', though this has no connection with any kind of race issue. He was rescued by the fact that he is a well-known homosexualist campaigner. The risible and the sinister contend with each other for the foreground in this anecdote.

In Britain in the same month the manager of the English football team got the sack for saying that physically handicapped people are suffering in this life for sins committed in an earlier one, a belief held by millions of people in Asia and, indeed, many hundreds of thousands in Britain itself. Then came the real British bombshell. In 1993 a young black Briton, Stephen Lawrence, had been murdered in South London by race bigots. There was a bungled police investigation and in face of public fury a report was commissioned under the leadership of Sir William Macpherson. It appeared, much of it written in the sub-Marxist jargon of PC, in late February 1999, accusing the whole of the London police force of 'institutional racism', and proposing a vast increase in the intrusive administrative structure of race relations in Britain, all without any decent evidence. It also advocated an extreme impressionism in the identification of racism, whereby, effectively, if A says B is a racist, B is.[86]

These are worrying facts. Even so, a certain caution is called for. In no sense should PC be thought of as having triumphed overall. Despite the distortions of recent years, no

---

85 Popper *op. cit.* Vol. 2, Chapter 23.
86 Leo McKinstry 'Macpherson was just a useful idiot', *Sunday Telegraph,* 28 February 1999.

one could reasonably say most American or British educational practice is anything like PC, let alone say this of our ordinary daily lives. What *is* true, however, is that other maladies, ones which contribute to PC itself, are far more prevalent. Consider contemporary sentimentality. Bruce Cooper and I have argued that education in America and Britain is shot through with a fatal sentimentality; and certainly PC can be seen as an extreme version of this fault, in which over-charged feelings about womanhood, non-whiteness and non-western culture, have driven reason and evidence from intellectual life.[87] Yet, most teachers are not ideologues. Most surely resist PC and like blandishments. They may, indeed, lead much of their working lives remote from PC. It is not these innocent teachers but the worst PC places and cases which concern the defenders of freedom. What requires pondering in all this is the question how far PC overlaps with totalitarian phenomena.

Does PC have totalitarian connections and if so, what are they?

Sentimentality is certainly integral to totalitarianism also, since the latter has turned precisely on sentimental abstractions about class and race.[88] Is PC then totalitarian? The idea has at times been challenged, even by resolute opponents of all socialist or adversarial thought. William McGowan, for example, reviewing Richard Bernstein's book on multiculturalism in the *Wall Street Journal*, praises it for its many examples of PC in action; but he distances himself from Bernstein's comparing PC with the French Terror or the Cultural Revolution, an exercise he finds 'needlessly portentous'.[89]

What, though, are the right words for PC? In many universities, American and British, something horribly new, intellectually and politically, is happening, something implacable and insistently intrusive. The core concerns are, indeed, race, sex, culture and sexual preference, but there is also an outer layer fixing on health, age, tobacco, the environment, hunting, the raising/transporting of livestock, the eating of meat and many

---

87 Cooper and O'Keeffe *op. cit.*
88 *Ibid.*, p. 60–61.
89 William McGowan 'A Politically Incorrect Study of PC', *Wall Street Journal*, 4 January 1995.

more. A new, alien intolerance surrounds the discussion and social management of all these. It is a commonplace that certain quarrels over these questions seem often to generate violence. This alien intolerance is so extreme that even a preliminary mapping of PC cannot be convincingly done unless we at least air its possible connections with modern totalitarian movements.

How may we answer McGowan? The Popperian rule is that one should always attack an argument first at its strongest point. McGowan's charge is initially very plausible. Indeed, once the general argument is conceived in a narrow way his case seems impregnable. Comparing PC with Communism or Nazism does raise grave difficulties. PC is fanatical ideologically, but very undeveloped politically. It is not killing anyone, for example. Quite understandably, then, some scholars or writers, even conservative ones, might indeed be sceptical of 'portentous' comparisons. After all, the modern attempt to create total control over other human beings has led to the worst mass murders of all time, and made our century uniquely repugnant. By comparison PC's attempt at a gross socialisation of mind seems small beer. It can make some decent people's lives intolerable, by blocking their books and promotions and even ruining their careers. These are insufferable affronts to a free society; but they are not Hitler or Stalin in action.

The McGowan argument is not finally compelling, however. It is a static assessment. The proper response to McGowan is to distinguish between the *potential* and the *realisation* of things. Anyone identifying PC as belonging to the totalitarian genus has to emphasise its *intrinsic character much more than its consequences*. The latter are not in the major league of wickedness. In practical terms they cannot be. PC's ideological bark does seem far worse than its consequential bite; and it is a philosophical commonplace that realised evil is worse than prospective evil. Nevertheless, movements are partly defined by their intrinsic character. An awkward question for McGowan is this: was the *essence* of Communism different in 1916 or of Nazism in 1932 from what followed? To say PC is not totalitarian is like saying the British National Front is not totalitarian simply because it has not achieved power. It is surely the intentions and the moral outlook of PC which count most in our evaluation. Anyway, in various versions PC *has* gained partial control of our quotidien arrangements, with the very adverse results we have just been discussing.

Another counterfactual question McGowan should consider concerns the consequences which would flow from the realisation of what certain Africanists and feminists now propose. PC Mark 1 wanted men and whites and the shades of Dante and Shakespeare to atone for past oppressions, and to make some space for women, blacks and non-European cultures in our curriculum. None of this seems very convincing, as I have argued elsewhere.[90] PC Mark 2, however, is terrifying in its implications. It wants to fortify beyond measure the divisions which already split the human race.

The question, it should be noted, is not whether all blacks and whites will be made to live separately, not whether lesbianism will be universalised. It is: what would occur if PC groups were able to institutionalise these gross ideas – to try them out? O'Sullivan points out that it is the attempted application of such extreme ideas which is so menacing.[91] They seem to embody horrors potentially as dire as those of totalitarianism realised. What would a world where the ideas that all whites are wicked or all males rapists were institutionalised, actually be like? We do not precisely know; but the vision certainly belongs in the Holocaust, Gulag and Cultural Revolution ascendancy. These terrible events too were once only uncertain and unworked out ideas held by cranks and misfits. Even in aspiration these divisive ideas are totalitarian, simply because it would not be possible to set about creating racial or sexual or cultural separation without a totalitarian apparatus of government.

PC: the Nazi connection

More surprising than McGowan's misleading common sense, is the failure of PC's opponents to spot what kind of totalitarianism PC resembles. In fact, 'surprising' is too weak. 'Extraordinary' would be better. If comparisons are carried out fairly, the results are startling. Let us concentrate on PC as an ideology. The claims it makes about race, sex and culture imply an utterly bleak and non-negotiable reality. In each case a hated enemy is identified – men, white people, Western culture – and identified as irredeemable. Men are seen as intellectually

---

90 O'Keeffe 'Multiculturalism and Cultural Literacy' *op. cit.*, see note 9 above.
91 O'Sullivan *op. cit.*

and affectively quite remote from women,[92] as are white people from blacks.[93] Non-European cultures are viewed as having nothing in common with mainstream European culture.[94] It is alleged that humans vary cognitively in terms of race, sex and culture, to such degree that we should think of white consciousness, science and art as utterly different from black mentality and thought, of the male mind as making no contact with the female mind and so on.[95]

All sense of common humanity is lost in this hateful thinking. The great truth that whatever divides humans, all people share in the seemingly unique powers and possibilities of our species, as well as in its burdens and limitations, that we all have in common the same mode of being in the world, is pushed aside by this intolerance.

We have heard something very like this malice before in our century. Not from Communists: they claimed, however hypocritically, that Communism would reconcile all human beings. Quite the opposite occurred, but at least in terms of presenting its credentials Communism was a universalist creed. PC reminds us, irresistibly, on the contrary, of Nazi ideology. The claim that men cannot coexist with women, or whites with blacks, is very like the claim that Germans cannot live with the *untermenschen*. The theses that men cannot live in harmony with women, or blacks with whites, are versions of ascriptive reasoning. PC is an ascriptive ideology, one which asserts congenital differences. However embryonically, it belongs to the totalitarianism of separation. As John O'Sullivan has said, '... the idea of culture as carried in the blood is closer to Nazism than to any democratic philosophy'.[96] Like Nazism and Fascism before it, PC has inherited from European romanticism a mania for separation. Like these movements PC retains the equality principle in a restricted form. Just as the Nazis wanted equality among Germans and for them alone, so the various currents of PC remain egalitarian for their chosen groups.

The Nazis and Fascists thought on a bigger scale. They sought to mould whole nations. PC's dream is big enough all the

---

92 Yates *op. cit.*, Chapter 3.
93 *Ibid.*
94 O'Sullivan *op. cit.*; Hughes *op. cit.*, Lecture 2.
95 Yates *op. cit.*, Chapter 3.
96 O'Sullivan *op. cit.*

same: the overthrow of inherited tradition in our intellectual world, that is to say the rejection of Judaeo-Christianity and the abandonment of the Enlightenment project, in crucial areas of academia.

McGowan would be on safer grounds if he said this totalitarian mission can never get near full realisation. This is probably right. O'Sullivan too thinks PC will fail though it will hurt us all in the process.[97] Even so, whatever PC's potential, it is already partly realised.

A hugely significant example: our ordinary vocabulary. Repeated emphasis has given us 'gender' for sex, 'gay' for homosexual and partner for spouse, for example, usages without a shred of justification. They serve no general interest, merely propitiating, temporarily, implacable hostilities. And some of the practical consequences of PC conventions are much worse even than the loss of innocent words. We all lose when people cannot express their views, even ones we find repulsive. Finn speaks of the 'Beirut syndrome' on some American campuses, as elements in the student body become irreconcilably alienated from each other.[98] This is a politics of separation on Nazi lines. Just as Nazism was a Marxist heresy, so PC has revised *neo-Marxist* and other egalitarian theorising. PC has been able to draw on half a century of mutating socialist peroration and agitation, most of it financed by the taxpayer. The next chapter will therefore take an extended look at a subject never yet given the attention it demands: the strange, still often unrecognised socialism of educational life in the free societies.

---

97 *Ibid.* O'Sullivan is presumably thinking of the costly efforts we will need to make to keep the PC mania at its present level and, once PC has failed, of the difficult repair job we will face. Doubtless, unknowable lunacies attend us in the future anyway.

98 Chester E. Finn Jr 'Can Our Colleges Fix our Schools?', *Academic Questions* Spring 1991.

3 | Socialist education in the free societies

Introduction

Western education systems involve socialist institutions and socialist ideas. In the union of the two is socialist praxis (a union of theory and practice), a grasp of which is needed for understanding intellectual and cultural transmission in societies like ours. The claim that education in Britain and America is socialist, however, needs more than mere assertion. Many capitalist phenomena are also manifestly at work in our educational life. Indeed, the free enterprise adjacent to and also penetrating our schools and colleges and their supporting administrative structure is a *resource* as well as a threat to their socialism. The greater staying power of sectoral compared to general socialism can in good measure be explained by its coexistence with markets. Markets produce the taxable wealth and purchasable *matériel* which sectoral socialism requires. The attempts at fully socialist production, i.e. at going it alone, without this private enterprise dependency, have failed worldwide. Sectoral socialism within market economies, by contrast, lives on, with education its most notable instance, indeed its most dangerous one, since education is the main motor of socialist *ideas* in our societies.

The growing recognition of educational socialism

Recently scholars have increasingly recognised educational arrangements in countries like America and Britain as 'socialist'. They have usually concentrated on obvious institutional features: public finance and attenuation of markets. The most eminent of such observers is Milton Friedman.[99] In fact,

---

99 Milton Friedman and Rose Friedman *Free to Choose*. Secker and Warburg, 1980, Chapter 6, p. 154. Here the Friedmans speak of American education as 'an island of socialism in a free market sea'. In this Chapter 6, though advocating a voucher system, the Friedmans make plain that they favour

it is just as crucial to disentangle the socialist *ideas* of education.

These socialist ideas pervade education. The strongest is that most protean of concepts: equality. Like socialist institutions these ideas too coexist with non-socialist counterparts. The assumptions of our traditional civil order and élitist Western intellectual heritage continue to assert themselves. Nevertheless, a relentless tide of egalitarian conceits informs many contemporary intellectual ills.[100] People do not usually call them 'socialist'. In the USA they are known as 'liberal' and they are not usually called socialist even in Britain. Nevertheless, 'socialist' is the best word for them since they *are* egalitarian and egalitarianism is the very matrix of socialist ideology.

These ideas are dangerous both in their universalist form, when they propose Utopian equalities, and in their latest, separatist incarnations, where equality is reserved for insider groups like women, blacks and non-western cultures, everything male, white or western being derided and opposed as inferior or oppressive. This latest trend marks the real end of the Enlightenment in significant areas of western scholarly life. It favours ugly divisions in a world crying out for reconciliation.[101]

The mediocrity of socialist educational production

Whether the core problem is public funding or egalitarian ideology or a union of both, however, socialist education is mediocre. There is a sad underperformance from bottom to top of the American and British systems. These are now miserable hierarchies. As Chester Finn and David Frum – independently – agree, there is a whole chain of mediocrity involved in American

---

free state education at the point of use for lower income families, though they believe many would dip into their own reserves to 'top up' under a voucher régime. *Free to Choose* does, however, mark a significant moment in Milton Friedman's developing thought in matters educational. He had earlier referred to education in his famous *Capitalism and Freedom op. cit.* as 'nationalised'.

100 Yates *op. cit.* Yates's whole book is about the unstable but voracious egalitarianism which underlies PC and Affirmative Action. Certainly this is how Anne Wortham sees the book in her cogent introduction (pp. xiii–xiv).

101 *Ibid.*, Chapter 3; Hughes *op. cit.*, Lecture 2 'Multi Culti and its Discontents'. Hughes too has very effectively shown the instability of egalitarian ideologies, with their tendency to pass from making claims of equality to claims of superiority, e.g. modern feminism and modern Africanism.

education from start to finish, in which secondary education fills in the gaps left by elementary schools, and tertiary education often does the jobs the high school should have done.[102] In the British case the ideology of the primary school – mediated by teacher education – has had a disastrous effect on the whole system.[103]

Education is a hybrid: many market forces are at work

All the same, we are looking – we repeat – at a hybrid economic form. Like the mixed economies themselves education combines different productive modes, philosophies, ideologies and practices. There are marked financial and institutional variations, between and within nations. Students at publicly financed universities in America pay fees; British students did not till recently, and even now pay rather small ones. The families of children at American public schools buy their books; this does not happen in British state schools. American religious schools get no subsidy. Many British religious schools get most of their finance from the state.

These institutional differences raise philosophical and political issues, as in the American controversy over financing parochial schools. The root problems of education in both countries, are, indeed, intellectual and ideological as much as institutional. While rival ideas may coexist, they also clash, sometimes violently. An example is the old academic idea, reinforced by the civil order, and consistent also with modern labour markets, that intellectual life is essentially a competitive reckoning. This idea collides with the egalitarian stance of socialist ideology, also strongly present in manifold forms in our educational culture, a countervailing tendency to suppress competition, to scorn academic hierarchies and to seek various political transformations of intellectual life. This tension is the defining one in our intellectual life today and much will hang on whether and how it is resolved in the years to come.

Though public money and egalitarian ideas predominate, many market influences are apparent in our institutions of

---

102 Finn 'Can Our Colleges Fix Our Schools?' *op. cit.*; Frum *op. cit.*
103 See O'Keeffe 'Diligence Abandoned' *op. cit.* I have even heard talk in British universities about the 'student-centred curriculum' – a clear mimicry of the follies of primary education. See also O'Keeffe *The Wayward Elite op. cit.*

learning. Capitalism and its works have now made a direct educational appearance both in America and Britain, and, indeed, in all advanced societies. For example, there is a great deal of privately organised knowledge and skill transmission. Gareth Williams and Maureen Woodhall have charted some of this in the British case.[104] There is also a very extensive system of private tutoring in both countries covering mainstream curriculum and many other activities, such as the learning of music and coaching in various sports. This commercially managed transmission of knowledge has not received much attention from social science; but it must affect the public sector favourably – the latter's faults would be even more glaring save for this private rectification.

Moreover, a substantive market influence is increasingly present in the curricula of schools and even more in those of universities. Accountancy, business studies and management are just some of the examples in the latter case and instruction in IT happens at all levels.

In British university schools of education there is also at long last some interest in the way young children view economic and industrial questions. The School of Education at my own university, for instance, has a strong interest in the economic attitudes of very young children.[105]

A significant market influence is apparent managerially too. The increasingly important practices of educational auditing and line management simulate the world of private enterprise. Given that we live in predominantly capitalist societies, none of this seems surprising, and every American and British university now maintains an overt market-oriented administrative vocabulary: efficiency, cost-effectiveness, evaluations, mission statements, market strategies, appraisals, profiles. Perhaps such terminology is now *passé* in the commercial economy and education is behind the times in market terms. All the same, this language does reflect market influence and the tentative convergence of the private and public sectors.

Educational socialism is not, then, pure and undiluted. Our schools and colleges also reflect the influence of the market and élite intellectual traditions. Even so, just as with qualifications the American and British economies may be defined as

---

104 Gareth Williams and Maureen Woodhall *Independent Further Education*. Policy Studies Institute, 1979.

105 Please contact the author for details.

fundamentally *market economies*, so our education systems are fundamentally *socialist*.

The two socialisms of education in the free societies

I have said that educational socialism has two main aspects. There is first the 'institutional' socialism implied by publicly financed schools and colleges which are not profit-maximising and whose capital is not privately owned. These criteria typify most American and British education. Moreover, most 'private' schools are not 'capitalist' either. Their propensity to outperform state-dominated schools is not a function of free enterprise, though they *are* more responsive to parents than state schools are, because such parents pay directly and seek value for money. In this sense such schools are closer to the market than state schools are. They are rarely profit-making, however, in the sense of paying out income to shareholders.

The main difference is that private schools do not receive most of their finance from public sources and are relatively free from state control. One large twentieth-century lesson for posterity is that the state corrupts or enfeebles much of what it touches, education being no exception. Privately financed institutions mostly avoid this, even when, as is the norm, they are not profit-led, and even when, as in American parochial schools, they are less well funded than state schools.

In the event American and British primary and secondary schools are overwhelmingly dependent on public finance. This bias is especially heavy in the USA. Even in the tertiary sector public finance bears the heaviest burden in both countries, especially Britain. In Britain, there is only one private university, for example. Even in America, where there are many private universities, most tertiary education is publicly financed and private universities receive large subsidies.[106]

---

106 In 1995 the average tertiary institution in the USA sold $11,967 worth of education for $3,370. Daniel Casse and Bruno V. Manno 'The Cost and Price of College and the Value of Higher Education', *Academic Questions* 11(4), Fall 1998, pp. 42–44. The authors also say that the value of subsidies is declining and that this may make consumers of higher education more discriminating. *Ibid.*, p. 52. The authors say a college degree is still good value. They do not ask whether higher education finance in America (and in Britain the case is much the same) is justified in *social* terms, that is whether public funds in higher eduction, declining or not, are well used. To the extent that

Mass education in America and Britain is thus mostly state-provided and financed. Indeed, institutional socialism is the norm for education in *all* advanced societies. What matters for the study of wayward ideologies, is that the natural drift of 'state' institutions is towards monopoly or quasi-monopoly and an attendant misuse of resources.

The evolving ideologies of educational socialism

Some of the ideologies of the egalitarian tradition were tracked in the last chapter. Their history is a background to the racial, sexual and cultural themes of PC. 'Progressivism' equates childhood with adulthood. Affirmative Action in America, and Equal Opportunities and Special Needs in America and Britain, are essentially egalitarian endeavours, trying to equalise conditions and/or atone for past wrongs. So too 'animal rights' equalises human and non-human life and the green movement puts plants on the same level as people, though I would repeat that there are also justified versions of these concerns. Some such ideas, however, are foolish to start with. Unfortunately, innocence has betrayed us too. Certain well-intended ideas and once innocent versions of educational equality, such as the initially far from sinister idea of 'special needs', have turned out to be dangerous. The thinking behind special needs was often mawkish; but the real trouble was that its thoughts soon fell in with bad company, such as rightsology and moral relativism, themselves sub-Marxist residues. The resulting ideological mix and the vested interests generated, supplied some of the insidious impulses we find in PC, for instance what Yates shrewdly conceives as its quota-like aspects, the notion that any social group must always be proportionately represented in any serious activity or institution, such that failure for this to occur *ipso facto* entails oppression.[107]

Doubtless, few individuals hold all these views simultaneously. Millions convinced by Equal Opportunities, for example, might indignantly reject the label 'PC'. Many too, would find the green movement or animal rights excessive or absurd in many versions. These movements are all egalitarian ones,

---

education is publicly financed it is effectively part of the huge welfare spending of modern government. This has occurred despite clear evidence that education is first and foremost a private, rather than a public good.

107 Yates *op. cit.*, Chapter 2.

nevertheless, part of a tradition which at its worst, a worst which has often obtained, has proved unstable and voracious, caught up in widening circles of absurdity and menace.

On multiplying educational absurdities

Although PC views may seem outlandish, they stand in a long line of views many of which might well have seemed absurd at the time of their initiation. Their supporters slipped them into place and in time they came to seem reasonable to some people. One example among many: our grandparents would have thought ridiculous the idea that children are naturally good.[108] It expresses the claim that childhood and adulthood are 'equal', an idea effectively removing much of the significance of education. Even today many American and British parents would reject such an idea. Yet it has been institutionalised widely in America and Britain, with incalculable effects on educational methods, educability, social order, relations between age-groups and so on.[109]

The educational *synthesis* of the two socialisms has entrenched destructive interests and inspired many of the passions which now haunt and corrupt the free world, despite the fall of many of its overtly totalitarian enemies. We should not underestimate this praxis. Significant minorities now believe that all whites – or all men – are oppressors, that all cultures are equal or that all civilisation began in Africa and so on. Most of us see these ideas as absurd. Over decades, however, the standards of discussion have gradually been lowered, with the result that today various absurdities have some appeal. Moreover, what is now voluntarily professed by fairly small minorities bears an uncanny resemblance, in its absurdity if not its substantive content, to the mantras imposed on whole populations by the Communist societies. And in modern Africanism and separatist feminism the absurdities embraced resemble the claims of National Socialism even substantively.[110]

---

108 Cooper and O'Keeffe *op. cit.*, p. 59.
109 O'Keeffe *The Wayward Elite op. cit.*; Kramer *op. cit.* In fact a lot of crime and social distress today may be explained via the partial infantilising of the population which progressivism has secured. This cannot be measured but the circumstantial case is strong.
110 Talk about whites being ice-people and blacks sun-people is pretty much on the same level as Stalinist mantras or Mao's little red book, and even closer to Hitlerite prejudices.

Malfunctions and dysfunctions in socialist education

Overall, then, the socialist elements in education are more note-worthy than those reflecting the market or civil order. Indeed, educational shortfalls in the west are in some ways like those which discredited general socialism. Educational socialism too is marked by signal malfunctions and dysfunctions in economic activity.

Economic malfunctions are shortcomings in performance, where scarce resources are used inefficiently. An example from the old Communist societies was their notorious harvest deficits. People want good harvests and Communism did not deliver them. Economic dysfunctions, on the other hand, involve the use of resources for illegitimate purposes, ones without general public support. In Communist states these included the wide-spread police surveillance of the population, the teaching of Marxist propaganda as scientific truth and the waste of resources in an unwinnable arms race.

In a free society with socialist education the results are naturally far less dire. Nonetheless there are failures, not in the same degree, but in the same direction. One equivalent mal-function is mass illiteracy or innumeracy. The evidence for this is now quite overwhelming.[111] The best example of a comparable *dysfunction* is the teaching and practice of PC and related propa-ganda. These malfunctions and dysfunctions are the combined long-term effects of the two socialisms of education, smaller-scale analogues of the production deficits and intellectual dis-tortions of general socialism. They reflect producer-capture, the replacement of the spontaneously aggregated *demand* prefer-ences of citizen-consumers by the *supply* preferences of an ideological nomenklatura with a very different, intellectually corrupt, agenda.[112]

Indeed, the most salient feature of western education is the extent to which it is supply-led, unlike market economic life. The educational élites in America and Britain have immense

---

111 The question now both in the American and British contexts is *why* this should be than *whether.* See for American evidence Andrew J. Coulson *Market Education: The Unknown History.* Transaction, 1999, Chapter 6. Recent evidence from English schools is well presented in Marks *op. cit.*

112 I have called this nomenklatura the 'wayward élite'. See Notes 5 and 11 above.

power. No capitalist group enjoys anything like so much influence in its private commercial sphere, since capitalists have to obey the dictates of the market. The educational élite seeks above all to lay down what counts as knowledge, what counts as teaching and what counts as academic evaluation. A significant minority of its members make up a strong element in the PC leadership. Indeed, only in such a strongly socialist environment could a corruption like PC gain an initial grip, though it can fan out elsewhere subsequently, and indeed has done so.[113] PC and Affirmative Action and Equal Opportunities – to which PC is closely related – are weak mimicry, pale counterparts, of the Leninist poison which crippled Russia for 70 years.[114]

PC is not, then, an apparition from nowhere. It stands in a long line of febrile ideological complaint in an educational output undisciplined by the market. Across the decades the ideologies of socialism have been gradually filtered into education and society until many people have become habituated to them. This can be seen most readily in questions of vocabulary. The way in which 'gender' has replaced 'sex', the euphemism 'gay' displaced the neutral 'homosexual' and 'partner' been introduced to rebuke those who retain the quaint practice of heterosexual marriage, are the most obvious examples.

The conceptual and theoretical innovations underlying our various word changes are worse, however. The notion that children are naturally good, the idea that competition is inherently bad, the claim that it is wrong to separate children by intellectual ability, the belief that educated people should not be 'judgemental' about cultural outlooks other than their own, the contention that there is no such thing as intellectual or cultural superiority and the insistence that ordinary moral language cannot cope with sexual and racial prejudice: such absurdities have been taught by people mostly paid or subsidised by taxpayers. The **sociologism** proposing that male/female behaviour differences are all socially constructed *and* the utterly opposite **psychologism** that male/female cognition are unbridgeably distinct and mutually incomprehensible: such anti-civilisational

113 For some American reflection see Yates *op. cit.*, Chapter 1; for the British case see Halfon *op. cit.*

114 Alexander Solzhenitsyn 'The Relentless Cult of Novelty', *Salisbury Review* September 1993, p. 32.

oddities have been brought into society – sometimes drip-fed, sometimes by *blitzkrieg* – via school and college. The ground has been laid for at least a sizeable minority to be so primed ideologically that even PC ideas do not seem wild or dangerous.

Anti-'didacticism' and the growth of relativism have weakened the transmission of culture.[115] Victimology and deterministic critiques of individual responsibility have diminished our moral sense.[116] There has been an educationally led partial undermining of family, school, labour markets and law and order. A large section of the 'educated' middle classes lead the way here, though the most visible embodiment of this cynicism is found among the poorer and less informed members of society. They are, indeed, victims of other people's folly, though not in the sense found in standard victimology. It is a typical socialist result that the poor and the weak are the main losers from educational as from all economic inefficiency.[117]

The socialist educational disaster
and the indignant academe

When critics of mass education say it is a disaster, however, they do not mean that most people do very badly. The public would not tolerate this in an increasingly middle class society with a deep commitment to work and career. It would be an educational version of the general immiseration characterising only *predominantly socialist societies*. With the obvious and important exception of mass culture,[118] there is no general form

---

115 Hirsch *The Schools We Need: And Why We Don't Have Them op. cit.* Hirsch insists that hostility to direct instruction is *not grounded in research findings* (p. 173); Bloom *op. cit.* believed that relativism was the defining belief of American students of the humanities.

116 Yates *op. cit.*, Chapter 3.

117 O'Keeffe 'Multiculturalism and Cultural Literacy' *op. cit.*, pp. 75–79.

118 Roger Scruton has produced a brilliant anatomy of modern mass culture. See his *An Intelligent Person's Guide to Modern Culture*. Duckworth, 1998. The subject of mass culture has not been brought under the gaze of political economy, however, since the neo-Marxists wrongly associated it with the reproductive controls of capitalism. I have made a tentative attempt to explain mass culture as flowing from the moronising dialectic between lowest common denominator commerce and our education systems. See Dennis O'Keeffe 'The Philistine Trap' in Ralph Segalman (ed.) *Reclaiming the Family*, Paragon House, 1998. A plausible case can be made for the view that mass culture is the very *worst* constraint on successful education in countries like America and Britain today.

of immiseration to be found in any of the advanced market economies, where most economic deficits touch only minorities. Some of these are large. Nevertheless, in predominantly market societies there is a limit to the downward social convergence that can be achieved. The capitalist context puts a brake on the mischief educational and other welfare socialism can do.[119]

'Disaster' means average standards much lower than they should be, antinomian conviction far more marked than it should be, and a tail of intellectual underachievement hugely larger than we should tolerate. PC is simply our most dramatic educational dysfunction. It rests on a bedrock of malfunctions, on the empty defacted culture Allan Bloom used to bemoan[120] and on the failure to use the tried and trusted teaching methods E. D. Hirsch urges us to revive.[121] It expresses in hyperacute educational terms the socialist praxis. And at its most extreme what a weird socialism it now is in the west, witnessed at its most perplexing in a strangely caricatural form. The Marx-scenario presented by Brecht has been remaindered. Instead of grim, poverty-worn faces, and calloused hands bearing guns or billhooks, we now face the well-fed, sometimes even well-groomed rebels of the indignant modern academe. The anger is not proletarian. It cannot be squared with Marxism. How could it be, when mass education belongs to the public sector?[122]

---

119 Communism produced relatively classless tyrannies – a small deeply corrupt élite presiding over a largely undifferentiated and impoverished mass. General socialism causes downward convergence of standards. Unless there is a fundamental collapse of trade and production this downward convergence cannot happen in a modern market economy. The general trend in all advanced capitalist societies is towards upward social convergence.

120 Bloom *op. cit.*

121 Hirsch *The Schools We Need and Why We Don't Have Them op. cit.* See especially Chapter 7.

122 In fact both in America and Britain trades unions have long been much more militant in the public sector than the private. Antagonistic theories and practices in questions of class, race, sex and so on, are far more characteristic of the public sector than the private. Moreover in the American case, the teachers' unions have immense policy power, fighting every government move to rationalise educational arrangements and improve standards every inch of the way. See Myron Lieberman, Charlene Haar, and Leo Troy *The NEA and the AFT: Teachers' Unions in Power and Politics.* Pro-Active Publications, 1994. In the British case too, unions have joined with the rest of the educational establishment in resisting attempts at reform. The British

The motivation of PC people is not clear

It is not wholly clear what today's socialist intellectuals want. They harangue us with fugitive, ghostly theories, shifting neologisms and endless demands for our money. The more extreme factions, i.e. the various PC persuasions, want to control relations between the sexes and races. Some want actually to separate women from men, blacks from whites. Others want to displace the family and overturn the normality of heterosexual love. Success in any of these might entail the end of representative government and the rule of law. This would not trouble the advocates of PC. Affluence would also die, however, and this *would* bother them. It is one of their props. Only affluence could permit the self-indulgent theorising of today. And the mode of finance is crucial. Only affluence and *access to other people's money* as a socialist special case of affluence, could generate and sustain the writings of Foucault or Derrida. As Frum rightly observes, you could scarcely sustain an interest in such writings if there were not a vast tide of public finance washing around society.[123] The study of these nihilisms is a form of gross curricular consumption, a kind of ideological insider-trading. A culture given to preoccupation with such fare has access to more resources than sense as to how to use them. Indeed, authors of the Foucault ilk are largely playing games when they write. Maybe they do not know the danger.

Sadly, however, intentions and results may diverge. It is always folly to play with educational fire. I ask again whether the private economy or representative government could long survive widespread intellectual closure in the public outlook, as in the conviction that individual responsible agency is a figment or in the belief that our human world is ultimately meaningless. The mixed genius of innovation and repair which has marked the free enterprise and conservative democratic mentality might well tumble if men and women ceased to feel free or to find the world meaningful.

---

teaching unions specialise in that *sine qua non* of socialism, the suppression of information. They bitterly opposed parents' being able to find out about a school's comparative academic standing.

123 Frum *op. cit.*

The socialist principles of state education

How has this oddity of entrenched sectoral socialism come to be? The educational economy has strayed very far since mid-Victorian times from the spontaneous evolution of learning and culture it once manifested. Public finance, compulsory attendance and egalitarian ideology have taken American and British education very far from the paths of reason and sanity they once trod. The socialist principles of our education system have already been listed in Chapter 1. The socialist economic mode of education is given by: public money; suppression of competition and of the rational division of labour; demonetised transactions; moral hazard; fiscal illusion and the jockeying of élite groups for rents and position. State education is the most socialist and coercive branch of the welfare state in the advanced societies, the bulk of its services provided to compulsorily detained consumers on a 'free at the point of use' basis.

The political economy of this intellectual disaster has only recently been spotted and is still little understood. Counter-factual reflection suggests that it could not have happened if education had been governed directly by purchasing consumers. Bakunin was a better guide than Marx. He had divined that a general socialism would yield a general tyranny.[124] Though it has taken the intellectuals who run education in America and Britain almost a century and a half to create a writ-small educational equivalent of Sovietism, today the experience of PC shows that sectoral socialism can eventually produce a partial but nevertheless terrifying despotism.

Saving PC's bacon

The deadly potential of all this was long hidden from view. This is to some extent a matter of language. Socialist education is the socialism which still dare not speak its name, perhaps lest it go the same way as most of its siblings. In fact, however, educational arrangements benefit from their proximity to the market economy. Involvement with the monetary calculus imposes utilitarian constraints vital to the everyday life of civilisation. It is not banal to note that a public service in a lawful society must pay its private enterprise providers. This does not mean that public service is a good milieu for education or anything else. Real

---

124 Michael Bakunin *Statism and Anarchy*. Cambridge University Press, 1990.

efficiency can happen only when management is risking its own position by handling funds which are highly sensitive to misuse as well as to success, precisely because personal risk is involved. But in our societies educational management does make at least some contact with free enterprise.

The civil order of freedom also enters the education world with the teachers and children and students. The ideas and practices of tolerance and respect for persons and individuality, above all the rule of law – which have always been ruthlessly extirpated under general socialism – hang on in obstinate refusal of socialist ideology. Thus the stasis that has overcome most general socialism to date – at the time I write Cuba and North Korea stagger on – has been at the very least postponed in the case of sectoral socialism in the free societies. Indeed, education in the West seems unlikely ever to fall into an overall totalitarian posture. That posture belongs only to the PC 'patch'.

PC and its kindred ideologies have conquered a sizeable part of education and then spread outside, infecting law, the media and publishing and perhaps even influencing quotidian human relationships. Even so, the patch seems destined to remain such, a stomping ground for a sinister lobby-group politics, of a one-sided kind. This politics may be limited in potential, though it is clear that America and Britain are already less free societies than they were a few decades ago. This closure is what our socialist intellectuals have already managed for us.

This development reflects the socialist side of the mixed economy. The crucial point, however, is the durability of sectoral socialism. Hayek long ago pointed out that socialism does not have to be about state-based production. Institutional socialism also has a 'fiscal' version.[125]

It is true that the ownership of most schools in America and Britain by the state is a disaster in itself. Until property rights are involved in education – until there is a genuine educational bourgeoisie – it will never work really well.[126] At the same time,

125 Friedrich von Hayek *The Constitution of Liberty*. Routledge and Kegan Paul, 1960, Chapter 17, 'The Decline of Socialism and the Rise of the Welfare State'.
126 In the long run schools will have to be made viable by the establishment of genuine ownership of educational institutions. Just as a socialist interest has formed around socialist education, so we need a bourgeois interest to form in free enterprise education. An explicit discussion along these lines would have fortified even further James Tooley's fine book *Education Without the State*. Institute of Economic Affairs, 1996.

however, the schools and colleges do have the fabulous wealth of modern capitalism to draw on, first by way of taxation, and secondly by way of purchase. In an advantageous contingency which Communism did not enjoy, Western education finds that the production of books, computers and all its *matériel* can safely be left to the market. It tends to be only the core substantive activities of education, the ones conducted worst – teaching, grading, etc. – which constitute true socialist production. Private firms make most of the *matériel*. In this way, however inefficient socialist education may be, it is constantly in touch with systems which use resources efficiently. Though publicly financed education may at times run out of funds, there will always be private enterprise to meet its needs, when it is in a position to pay. It usually seems to be. Although public monies are inefficiently managed in our state bureaucracies compared to best market practice, they are doubtless models of probity compared to what used to happen in Communist societies.

American School Districts and British Local Education Authorities and individual schools and institutions of higher learning in both countries may sometimes be short of funds; but they are only in extreme cases unable to pay their bills. Fiscal socialism has shown itself durable in education as elsewhere. It was not dreamed up to be a parasite of capitalism; but that is what it is, and in survival though not in educational terms, a successful, tenacious one at that.

Indeed relationships also run from education to commerce. Socialist education establishes interests in the commercial economy. PC is by definition not a commercial phenomenon in the first instance. The main demands its ideologies make on society – the space they lay claim to in the university and school curriculum, the calls they put on teaching – are mostly not mediated through cash transactions. They do have an impact on the market, however. For decades progressive and socialist education have set up enormous interests in commercial publishing. Today there is an endless supply of nonsense books about race, 'gender' and multiculture, just as there is a large accumulation of writings promoting progressive education. Once the state sector endorses PC it finds niches in the capitalist society, in the sale of PC books and a growing PC component in entertainment. Such free enterprise is a sizeable oddity, dependent on a public 'base'.

Variations in socialist education

It must be said that the connections between socialist institutions and ideological socialism vary greatly, internationally and intranationally. For example, education in the Far East manifests very little ideological socialism anywhere. In the USA, on the other hand, as in the UK, the ideological socialism is much greater in some places than others. Thus in America and Britain PC is a larger presence in universities than in schools, and varies between universities and within universities. Above all, PC varies between subjects. Though this book has no space to pursue this complicated question, a good approximate rule is that the more secure the knowledge-base, the less likely is it to fall under PC colouration or management. The Sokal hoax showed how intrinsically difficult it is to subject mathematics and the hard sciences to PC treatment.[127] It is true that mathematics in schools is often misunderstood epistemologically. It is often taught as if it were an empirically based subject, to be picked up from experience. In the settled contexts of upper secondary and university education, however, its logical status continues in secure recognition. This contrasts with all the humanities subjects which are under assault from their earliest introduction to post-doctoral seminars.

In the education systems in the rich market economies of the orient, even the humanities and social sciences have proved impervious to the PC bacterium. It is important, however, that a misunderstanding be cleared up. Japanese and Singaporean schools are *not* economically efficient. Socialised production can never be so. It is simply that in the relative absence of socialist ideology in such schools, they are much less *inefficient* than ours. In fact, it is only in the advanced societies of predominantly white race that many senior, influential educational personnel – certainly in America and Britain – are dedicated advocates of ideological socialism, of which PC is the most advanced and extreme form. The paradox of America is that this socialism of ideological type is stronger there than anywhere else in the free world, though the free enterprise economy is also stronger in America than anywhere else on earth. Unfortunately, the widespread use of the word 'liberalism' has served to mislead the

---

127 Paul A. Boghossian 'What the Sokal Hoax Ought to Teach Us', *Times Literary Supplement,* 13 December 1996, pp. 14–15.

63

American people as to the threat to their way of life much of their education now constitutes.

The core intellectual error in America and Britain was the failure of the sociologists to understand our educational arrangements. The intellectuals of sociology, through ignorance more than malice in my view, were the worst offenders. This brings us to that most disreputable and yet mischievously successful paradigm of modern social science: the neo-Marxist sociology of education.

Neo-Marxist education theories were the opposite of the truth

The worst result of the 20 year reign of neo-Marxist sociology of education in America and Britain was that it held up for so long the understanding of the socialist educational arrangements under which we labour. Even now there is little sign that sociologists have woken up to this. Both American and British sociology of education, until their recent, virtually total silence on the matter, were obsessed for years with the capitalism/education reproduction model. It did not seem to dawn on M. F. D. Young,[128] Sam Bowles and Herb Gintis[129] or Michael Apple,[130] and a lot of other writers that the agency whose 'capitalist' functions they were so keen to identify was in fact a socialist arrangement.[131]

Future historians of thought will have to explain in detail the sad tale. Briefly, though, we can say without exaggeration that the sociologists themselves ruined their specialism. The economic ignorance of most American and British sociologists, for example, surpasses even their philosophical and historical deficits. Their error in the case of education lay in trying to reduce it to the power-relations of capitalism. In truth, the dominant power in education lies with its own internal élite.[132]

---

128 Young *op. cit.* This was the most influential British text dealing with the sociology of knowledge. It was incoherent intellectually but not in fact very 'Marxist'.

129 Bowles and Gintis *Schooling in Capitalist America op. cit.*

130 Michael W. Apple is a prolific writer. See his *Education and Power*. Routledge and Kegan Paul, 1995.

131 O'Keeffe 'The Name of the Game is Weber' *op. cit.*

132 Bowles and Gintis in *Schooling in Capitalist America op. cit.* insist that education is a capitalist tool. Their vast 'evidence' does not remotely justify this claim. What is wrong with the view that those who seem to be running

Neo-Marxism was never convincing in any version. In successful modern economies, where wealth is not a zero-sum game, where hard effort and scarce talent are mostly well rewarded, propositions about the 'ruling class' lose conviction very swiftly. Weakening by the mid-1980s, neo-Marxism had lost all authority by the early 1990s. Its advocates seem to have gone down with the Communist ship whose course and colours they often claimed to repudiate. There matters stand, save for a few melancholy Marxisant dinosaurs and some unconvincing excursions into Post-Modernism. Marxism is dead now. Lasch was right that it is no longer a major force in intellectual radicalism.[133] And as we noted in the previous chapter, PC is closer to Nazism than to Marxism, though it was also suggested that PC began as a heresy of neo-Marxist theorising, much as Paul Johnson has asserted that Fascism and Nazism are heresies of Marxism proper.[134]

The central claim of neo-Marxist education theory, as to what education does in a capitalist economy, is at one level unexceptional. Marxists refer to 'the reproduction of capitalist power', while conventional economists will prefer 'meeting the demands of the labour market'. The latter is a more accurate, less tendentious rendition of the former. Education must indeed meet the imperatives of the division of labour, for most people. There would be mass revolt if it did not. How could we enforce compulsory attendance if there were no instrumental payoff?

Former neo-Marxists have either been oddly silent in recent years or changed their preoccupations, often in the direction of the new obscurantisms of Post-Modernism. Some have even embraced PC. For whatever reason neo-Marxism fell, however, there has been no apology from any of its exponents about all the time they wasted in its exposition and all the students they

---

education, are, indeed, doing so? Why should we depart from the old notion that things are what they are and not something else? Bowles and Gintis are officially *economists* rather than sociologists. Most of their work is bad *sociology*. Can we trust them even as economists though? In *Schooling in Capitalist America* they argue that educated labour is 'productive but not scarce'. This is the purest economic illiteracy. See Dennis J. O'Keeffe 'Profit and Control: the Bowles and Gintis Thesis', *Journal of Curriculum Studies* September 1978.

133 Lasch *op. cit.*

134 For the likenesses between the various totalitarianisms see Paul Johnson *Modern Times: A History of the World from the 1920s to the 1990s.* Phoenix, 1996, Chapter 8 'The Devils', and also p. 102.

so grossly misled. Like all Marxism, neo-Marxist education theory was always deeply flawed. It suffered in particular from a fallacy of composition. It was assumed that since the economic system in general terms was identifiable as a market one, then the various parts of the society must be capitalist too. Hence Louis Althusser's suggestion that capitalist power in France operated via the 'capitalist education system'.[135] A similar argument came from Bowles and Gintis in an American version[136] and as late as 1990 Herbert Gintis was still talking about 'capitalist education'.[137]

The scholarship of error

Whole international choirs of scholarship for years sang of the capitalist character of our educational arrangements in the countries of the free world. This was as wide of the mark as that other great solecism of contemporary social science, the failure to grasp that Nazism and Fascism were fundamentally socialist phenomena.[138] Economic science was, by contrast, much less infected. Few economists claimed that education was about the reproduction of bourgeois power. Even among the economists, however, there was little sense of the discontinuities – the unexpected oddities and disappointing inefficiency – caused by the fact that our educational arrangements are not fundamentally capitalist.[139] The prevailing counterfactual analysis in sociology of education was wrong. It is not capitalism in the wider economy which is problematic, but the socialism of our schools and colleges. The task of righting this intellectual solecism has only recently begun.[140] A preliminary contribution to this correction will be our task in Chapter 4.

---

135 Louis Althusser 'Ideology and Ideological State Apparatuses' in Ben Cosin (ed.) *Education, Structure and Society*. Penguin, 1972.

136 Bowles and Gintis *Schooling in Capitalist America op. cit.*

137 Herbert Gintis in *British Journal of Sociology of Education,* Review Symposium 12(3), 1991, p. 383. The work reviewed was Chubb and Moe *op. cit.* It is hard to imagine a more shoddy review than this by the brilliant, mercurial Gintis. He should make a clean break with Marxism, like Koestler's.

138 Paul Johnson *op. cit.*

139 Dennis O'Keeffe 'Market Capitalism and Nationalised School' in B. Davies (ed.) *The State of Schooling*, Educational Analysis, Spring 1981.

140 Seldon *Reprivatising Welfare After the Lost Century op. cit.*

4 | Capitalism, socialism and PC: a counterfactual analysis

Introduction

Since the advent of compulsory education in America and Britain, there has been a gradually widening socialism in our academic arrangements, especially in primary and secondary schooling. To the inherently inefficient system originally constituted by compulsory attendance and public finance, successive layers of destructive egalitarian ideology have been added, especially since the 1960s.

Education is the most important part of any modern economy. Yet in America and Britain it is mired in public finance and burdened with 'equality', in various applications, as its governing principle. Thus it lacks the focus on accurate calculation which markets have. Many educational managers pursue the fantasy of equality. Were excellence their goal, they would be identifying *inequalities*. The financial context of this error is the careless use of resources. The moral hazard inherent in the spending of other people's money ensnares education inexorably. The financial risks of any policy for schools or colleges, any curricular or pedagogic innovation, are shunted sideways on to taxpayers. The result is a gross irresponsibility, embracing government, central and local, as well as individual schools and teachers.

Our socialist educational ways are fortified today by intrusive bureaucracy. Bureaucratic centralism is apparent in education in both countries, though in the USA mostly at state level, whereas in Britain most education – even tertiary education – is now centrally bureaucratised on a scale to warm the heart of a Lenin. Public finance and egalitarian ideology intertwine, endorsing and reinforcing each other, and bureaucratisation is advisedly calculated to enhance further the powers of providers and diminish the discretion of consumers.

It is truly strange how long it has taken for this socialism to be recognised. In the event, socialist educational production in the West has some fascinating – and alarming – similarities with educational and other production under general socialism. As we shall see, however, it also manifests some important differences.

One growing similarity is the alienation between the masses and the élites. Until the Second World War, or even the 1960s, there was a fair agreement between educators and public. As leadership has become more socialist (US 'liberal') in both countries, this consensus has shattered. We can detect this leadership bias not by listing socialist enthusiasts but by considering policies. Our élites have for 40 years been trying out their fantasies at public expense, dumbing down substance and standards in a deliberate homogenisation of output, one eventually involving a huge, frightening tail of underachievement.

We have been ill served. William Bennett was right to complain some years ago that it was as if an 'act of war' had been declared on the American people.[141] This could just as truly have been said of the British. Our large, mischievous expertocracies have diminished teacher authority. It is these experts who offend most. Obsessed with sentimental ideologies, impervious to correction and public opinion, they instantiate the proliferating power of the state, an enhanced position for rent-seekers and a growing and bureaucratised subversion of cultural and intellectual activity.

The subversive calculus of public funds

When the great J. A. Schumpeter observed that advanced societies tend to reward antinomian thought, he did not elaborate this important insight formally.[142] Nor did he note that as well as dysfunctional ideas, antisocial behaviour is sometimes encouraged. In particular he did not anticipate William Allen's trenchant observation that middle-class antinomianism and the ocular violence and criminality of the poorer strata in our society are intimately connected. As Allen puts it, in a world in which morality is seen as purely personal and arbitrary, we

---

141 William J. Bennett *et al.*, *A Nation at Risk*. National Commission on Excellence in Education, Washington DC, 1983.
142 Joseph A. Schumpeter *Capitalism, Socialism and Democracy*. Allen and Unwin, 1942.

have been 'deprived of every opportunity to apply the levers of duty and shame as regulators of human conduct'.[143]

Schumpeter did not specify how radical ideology is promoted, much less relate the matter to finance, private or public. Later, when Paul Johnson produced his celebrated history of our century, he echoed Schumpeter's shrewd observation and tightened it somewhat, fastening his gaze on education. His view is that mass education in free societies – his example is the American one – is a source more of disorder than consensus. He does not challenge Schumpeter's view that radicalism is a runaway version of the freedoms capitalism bestows.[144] Yet he does make it plain that American education, rather than winnowing excesses, has been naively permitted to absorb and intensify all the worst conceits conjured up. Educational administrators displayed the most reprehensible cowardice in the face of antinomian threats. Indeed, as Johnson puts it, '[t]he 'campus riot' became part of the college culture, as university presidents compromised, surrendered or abdicated'.[145]

Johnson improves on Schumpeter as to the locus of perverse thought. He too fails, however, to say anything about the finance of 'radical' thinking. And there for the most part matters have stood. We know about the temptations of public finance. We know about intellectual corruption. Yet scholarship has not much linked the two. Now, fortunately, in the American case, David Frum has produced a brilliant short essay on the corruptions which surround public money in general, arguing that mass, long-term welfare dependency and much of the ideological corruption of American life, relate to the trillions of dollars now swilling around the public sector.[146]

---

143 W. B. Allen 'The Fear of Disrepute' in Digby Anderson (ed.) *This Will Hurt.* Social Affairs Unit, 1995, p. 137. Allen does not use quite the strong nouns – antinomianism and nihilism – which occur to me. But he does relate the displacement of moral responsibility and the once-crucial sense of shame by materialist and environmental explanations and he does identify the moral poverty of managerial élites and their recourse to cash handouts and other public expenditure. The moral debilitation he explains – a moral collapse of intellect among the educated and in behaviour by the poor, fits my words perfectly.

144 Paul Johnson *op. cit.*, pp. 641–645.

145 *Ibid.* p. 643

146 Frum *op. cit.*

Public money, not the obsessions of ideologues – the problem Frum says that Hilton Kramer, Bill Bennett and Midge Decter have all so roundly and properly indicted[147] – is the key fact for Frum. Public finance is the independent variable. It is the fiscal and consequently curricular space provided for wayward thought by taxpayers' dollars which Frum sees as especially remiss.[148]

For Frum corruption is corruption is corruption. His essay is about welfare dependency and wayward ideologies as versions thereof, their likenesses taken for granted, subsumed in his under-standing of the moral hazards of the public purse. His approach could be more explicit still if he endorsed Allen's view that your middle-class intellectual explaining morality away, definitely corresponds to your lower-class thug.[149] Theirs are two versions of the same malady. Welfare dependency too is a malpractice with its ideological defence built in. Many academics deny or defend such dependency.[150] Others teach the nihilism whose visible demonstration comes from unschooled youths.[151]

Welfare dependants and their defenders are sustained from the same source: the much-abused taxpayer. And the sorts of people who tell you there is no welfare culture, or that the one-parent family is not dysfunctional, are also the kind who support PC generally, or at any rate certain of its tributary currents.

Intellectual evolution in public choice style

A theoretical evolution of growing explanatory force *vis-à-vis* insidious ideologies is apparent in the line from Schumpeter to Johnson and Frum. From the observation that our societies often treat ideological rebels well (Schumpeter), to the more specific hypothesis that academic arrangements can promote subver-sion (Johnson), we now move to a tighter, specifically financial

---

147 *Ibid.*, p. 28.
148 In fiscal year 1992 the US government spent nearly $1.5 trillion – a sum equal to the gross national product of Germany. *Ibid.*, p. 27.
149 Allen *op. cit.*
150 Danziger *op. cit.* For a compendious demolition of this kind of argument see Ralph Segalman 'The Underclass Re-Visited: Causes and Solutions' in David Marsland (ed.) *Work and Employment*. Paragon, 1994.
151 Allen *op. cit.*

formulation (Frum), which begins to take on the lineaments of a theory. The linking of intellectual determinism (as in PC) and lower-class criminality strengthens the case.

This whole ensemble can be linked to the public sector, the finance of the latter treated as the independent variable, though as so often in the relationships uncovered by social science, one whose effects are of a probabilistic rather than mechanistic kind. Public finance is always inefficient, as Chapter 3 argued, but for that inefficiency also to take the special form of ideological corruption, an auxiliary hypothesis has to be added. There have also to be present, adversarial or antinomian currents of thought. The origin of these lies outside economic life and also long predates mass education or the public finance of such education. Lasch has argued that the meaningless nature of the world and the hopeless alienation of human existence are ancient ideas.[152] Norman Cohn has shown how antinomian and egalitarian fundamentalism also predates modernity.[153]

PC is a psychological component of rent-seeking

The point though, is where all this disruption is to be found today. Socialist ideology in general, and its current culmination, PC, in particular, are part of the mind-set of certain predominantly public sector interests, a large element in the pyschological composition of their rent-seeking. The whole series of disruptive innovations from child-centred education to PC were brought in not for their intrinsic worth but to flatter this higher education élite and enact its ideologies. More precisely: *PC and multiculturalism are the ideological face of public choice.* Yates compares the worst gurus to the Nazis.[154] In fact, Caesarean comparisons fit people like Stanley Fish better, his preposterous claim that he can bend first-class academics to his will and his remarks about his narcissistic self-fixation – 'I'm fascinated by my own will' – recalling in their vanity the Caesars more than Hitler, and Caligula or Nero more than Julius.[155]

What permits a talented scholar to offend against ordinary decencies? The insights of public choice are precisely relevant

152 Lasch *op. cit.*, Chapter 13.
153 Norman Cohn *The Pursuit of the Millennium*. Paladin, 1970.
154 Yates *op. cit.*, Chapter 3.
155 Stanley Fish is alleged to have said he is fascinated by his own will and likes to dominate other academics. Yates *op. cit.*, pp. 67–68.

here. PC benefits from the kind of imbalance public choice theory has taught us to observe: those who favour PC are few; but their powers and determination are intense. Many, perhaps most of those who oppose, are weakly opposed, and care about other things more. Thus people only a step away from what most of us would see as deranged can get away with it.

A major advance in understanding radical ideology

Overall, some originally rather disparate thoughts now combine in a major advance in our understanding. That easy public money gives you welfare dependency is long established. Criminal dispositions constitute a significant subset of such dependency. We now add that public finance also gives you deracinated intellectuals anxious to defend dependency, one-parent families, etc., as well as to promote antisocial thought of the PC type, including the idea that much of what most of us take to be crime or deviance – or truth, or beauty or meaningfulness – is not such.

The counterfactual hypothesis radiating through the case is: *in the absence of public funds the growth of destructive ideologies would have been far less likely.* The public choice theorists have shown how the American state has been suborned for purposes of private rents.[156] We can go further, following Frum in seeing state education in America – and the same would apply to Britain – as the key locus for the present subversion of intellectual and moral life in that country.

If these fads do not need public finance why do they ask for it?

The hesitancy with which the thesis sketched here has emerged is perhaps surprising. Many tendentious fads need public resources. Their representatives endlessly plead for our funds. They would scarcely do so if they did not find them useful. Common sense may at times be problematic; but it has huge appeal in cases such as PC and its background stages and rages. Could the dangerous initiatives of sex education and other forms of 'values-clarification', brilliantly indicted by Killpatrick,[157]

---

156 J. M. Buchanan *et al.* (eds) *Towards a Theory of Rent-Seeking Society.* Texas A&M University Press, 1980.
157 William Killpatrick *Why Johnny Can't Tell Right from Wrong.* Simon and Schuster, 1993.

have been mounted without public funds? Would many parents, before the long years of supply-led propaganda, have paid straight cash for children to be taught to call husbands and wives 'partners' and see sexual activity only in terms of self-gratification and prudence? Would people have directly surrendered scarce income to have children urged to 'negotiate' the moral order? In fact, modern radicalism and progressivism have needed and used an extensive publicly financed network of institutions, especially mass education.

Modern socialist ideology combines intellectual exaggeration and distortion with social destruction. It has rarely been probed in the fiscal terms needed to do it justice. Private money can chase wayward causes. Rich people are sometimes wicked. Nevertheless, the perverse ideologies so powerful in America and Britain owe their main development to public institutions and finance, a view in no way overturned by the observation, in relation to the American genesis of the phenomenon, that much of the early running for PC came from private universities or the giant charitable foundations.

A number of rejoinders can be made to this counterclaim, despite its *prima facie* truth. Though charitable foundations deploy funds whose origin is capitalist, these are in no sense managed *vis-à-vis* any market logic. The capture of their boards by radical ideology has turned them into socialist treasure troves,[158] an argument which also applies to some foundations in Britain. A similar case could be made in Britain for the operations of the National Lottery. Furthermore, even the most élite universities receive massive public finance. This is even more true of Britain than America. Only a tiny minority of educational institutions at any level are profit-maximising. Most educational institutions need not even show a wise use of their funds.

PC is only the latest, most exotic layer of socialist thought

Above all the extent and intensity of socialist educational ideas have to be noted. PC is only the latest, most exotic layer of socialist thought. Its main home is in certain university

---

158 Finn 'Giving it Away' *op. cit.*

departments. It sits, however, at the apex of an extensive, gradually accumulating ideological structure which has characterised much of elementary and secondary education too for decades. It also rests on a very large institutional base: Equal Opportunities and Affirmative Action, Special Needs and all the other egalitarian interventionist programmes. Yates has shown how these ideas and structures intertwine with PC.[159] In such developments ideology is the drive and public finance the facilitator. The process has been going on for years. The comprehensive secondary school in Britain, and the common high school in America, are just such socialist (egalitarian) phenomena, institutional forms indelibly shaped by ideology.[160]

The two-edged nature of modernity

The crucial thought for civilisation, however, is the two-edged nature of modernity. Our publicly financed mass education, with its peculiar susceptibility to producer-capture, offers an unprecedented means for supporters of perverse convictions to spread them, separately or in unison.[161] At the same time the success of the privately financed economy and a vigorous civil order tend to check them, eventually remaindering the large-scale radicalism (e.g. Communism) and containing or marginalising the intellectual despair, cynicism and suspiciousness (of Foucault, Derrida and the like). If this sounds like an ideological tug-of-war for the souls of our young people, then I would say the comparison neatly catches the grating contradictions of our intellectual arrangements.

---

159 Yates *op.cit.*, Chapter 2. Britain is blessed in not having Affirmative Action, but only its weaker brethren, Equal Opportunities and Special Needs.

160 Despite their many failings these schools are fanatically defended in America and Britain. Not only are they publicly financed; they also institutionalise the view that the whole normal range of abilities can and should be catered for by the same institutions. Many of their supporters indeed maintain that there should be no élite institutions. See Cooper and O'Keeffe *op. cit.*

161 It may be doubted whether there was a conspiracy. Socialist intellectuals have used education as a means of getting their ideological programme set up, however.

Under public finance dubious ideologies can be imposed

Many activities of modern education would be hard to sell on a private basis. Under public finance the huge advantage for the supplying caste is that these activities can be imposed. Over the years the curricular and pedagogic landscape has bit by bit been advisedly transformed. The outlandish is at first slid in arbitrarily and then in some cases normalised. People may in time forget it was ever outlandish.

Most such innovations belong to the political/egalitarian persuasion. Others are technical errors. Coulson says, for example, that phonetically based teaching of reading has been displaced in America for a century, a disastrous technical wrong turn.[162] Tom Burkard notes that *look-and-say* took hold in Britain between the wars.[163] This has left millions illiterate. In both societies the teaching of mathematics has been a comparable failure.[164]

In any case, the technical and the ideological are connected. Look-and-say reading and the dropping of multiplication tables can both be seen as sentimental attempts at lightening life's grim burden, at equalising adulthood and childhood by abandoning painful rites of passage between them. The result is that millions of Americans and Britons today cannot read or number. Similarly, attacks on rote learning have led to much of the present generation not having done any. Likewise, long-standing indifference or hostility to high standards have left many people with low ones. More recently comparable attitudes to high culture have abandoned the arts to the mercy of philistines and anti-nomians.[165]

Things are no better on the moral front. Long years of 'progressive' discipline have weakened moral life. For decades public finance has permitted the (initially) supply-led levering into place of destructive notions such as the natural goodness of

---

162 Coulson *op. cit.*, pp. 160–168.
163 Tom Burkard *The End of Illiteracy: The Holy Grail of Clackmannanshire* CPS. 1999, pp. 4–5.
164 For the American case see Coulson *op. cit.*, pp. 157–160. For a damning indictment of the contemporary teaching of mathematics in English schools, see Marks *op. cit.*, pp. 7–8.
165 Scruton *An Intelligent Person's Guide to Modern Culture op. cit.*; O'Keeffe 'The Philistine Trap' *op. cit.*

children, the spontaneous nature of all worthwhile cognition and the cruelty of severe discipline of the young. Years of university (and some school) teachers proclaiming men sexist and whites racist and Western culture at best provincial and at worst oppressive, result in lots of people professing beliefs that affront the majority today and would have astounded virtually all our forebears. Certainly, as Allan Bloom observed, someone has been telling our young people that all values are 'relative'.[166]

Such ideas were mostly acquired in institutions of formal learning and in America and Britain this usually means public funds were involved. The follies of pre-university education were followed and paralleled in initially restricted and experimental contexts in higher education by the building block assertions of PC: racist whites, sexist men, Eurocentric culture. These conceits were rapidly filtered down to earlier stages, by way of teacher education. [167]

In all this the élite is indulging itself, acting out sometimes guilty or envious and always destructive fantasies. Successive waves of egalitarian experimentation have swept across the various levels of American and British education in the twentieth century, especially in the second half. We may counterfactually presume that these must have altered the educational experience substantively. Certainly the net effects have lately included large minorities adopting PC postures. For this to be achievable, it was crucial that the students at the various stages be cognitively different from what traditional teaching would have secured.

To take one example: children who have been separated by intellectual ability will inevitably experience school – and the world – differently from those who have not. The latter will respect intellectual hierarchy less and be less bound by academic tradition. To take another: children taught the value of silence will see authority differently from those usually allowed to talk. Public finance of education, when it is assumed that educational leadership is competent, permits the imposition of outlandish ideas. Combined as it usually is with lack of exit for dissatisfied consumers, it has facilitated the bedding in of these ideas

---

166 Bloom *op. cit.*
167 Kramer *op. cit.*; O'Keeffe *The Wayward Elite op. cit.*; Finn 'Can Our Colleges Fix our Schools?' *op. cit.*

simultaneously with the dumbing down of the students. Intelligence, authority and effort have been gradually weakened as governing ideas. Students become at once more cynical about tradition and credulous about innovation. They are thus easier prey to false scholarship.

We are indebted to those who have pointed to the dumbing down. Neither Bloom[168] nor Hirsch[169] draws attention, however, to the publicly financed character of the schools. Nor does Chester Finn, though he identifies teacher education as the main offender in the system.[170] He is right; though teacher education's role is more in terms of relaying falsehoods than originating or consolidating them.[171] The thinking, such as it is, happens in humanities and social science departments and like venues. But the whole system is infected, though in varying degree. In particular, decades of relativism deprecate all the traditional canons of scholarship and ethical life.

We have moved across the years from progressive education to the extravagances of PC. Any major breaks in this sequence of increasingly phantasmagorical character – owing to shortages of finance for example – might have stopped the whole caravan. The crucial counterfactual point is that the whole thing would not have been manageable without recourse to public monies. *There would not have been sufficient private demand.*

The curriculum on offer is not a proper one, since the public have been deliberately taught not to understand it. Society is now rather easy prey to a supply-led and in some instances deeply subversive curriculum. Demarketised education, a socialist praxis incorporated also in teacher preparation and educational research, has in time produced a managerial élite exactly along the lines cherished by Lenin and foreseen with such dread by Bakunin[172] and Majachski.[173] This élite is very

---

168 Bloom *op. cit.*
169 Hirsch *Cultural Literacy: What Every American Needs to Know op. cit.*
170 Finn 'Can Our Colleges Fix our Schools?' *op. cit.*, pp. 62–66.
171 Finn also ignores the infantilising primary influence on secondary and higher education. See O'Keeffe *The Wayward Elite op. cit.*
172 Bakunin *op. cit.*
173 Machajski was an obscure Pole whose texts (in Russian) remain mostly untranslated. He presciently saw that the rule of the intellectuals was a terrible tyranny. See Marshall Shatz 'Jan Waclaw Machajski: The Conspiracy of the Intellectuals'. *Survey* January 1967.

powerful in social science, in humanities and the teaching of morality, at university and pre-university levels.

Modern educationalists mostly view this new stratum in an accepting spirit. They do not indict its obfuscations although these result in lots of people's simply not knowing what is going on. Basil Bernstein's well known essay on pedagogic styles affects a quite typical studied neutrality.[174] His text baldly admits that the 'experts' have rendered much of what happens in British classrooms unintelligible to non-specialists. This seems not to dismay him in the least. He also notices, shrewdly, that these experts 'interrupt' the bourgeois order, with their 'progressive' doctrines and hostility to hierarchies other than those specified in their own **gnosis**. The fact that such interruption means unnecessary proletarian retardation for many people seems not to faze him at all.

The economics of the education system overall

The perpetuating mechanisms of this economic disaster are ones long familiar to neo-Classical or Austrian perspectives: lack of information, lack of exit, lack of choice, weak or non-existent auditing of production, etc. Public money in state institutions was the background facilitator of all this error, compounded by defiant ideologies. Intellectual corruption is a dependent artefact of tax-revenues, a dependence likely to characterise any future antinomian movements.

The New Testament is misleading in its occasional hostility to private wealth. Public, not private funds are Hell's most effective earthly fuel. After large-scale demonstrations of this truth from Stalin and Hitler we now get more provincial and less ambitious versions of the same from Western education. Admittedly, no one should doubt that private funds are corruptible too. The relentless shelfloads of PC books in the bookshops show that there is a gullible clientèle. Lots of affluent people are now more or less PC. For this tame audience those who teach the doctrines are heavily indebted, however, to public finance, past and present. The taxpayer's wealth has played a dominant part in the long-term formation of this gullibility. It is this which most offends. PC would still be vile if it were all

---

174 Basil Bernstein 'Class and Pedagogies: Visible and Invisible' in *Class, Codes and Control* Vol. 3. Routledge and Kegan Paul, 1975, pp. 116–156.

privately financed. The case would be more surprising and enigmatic, however, since we would not be able to link PC with those institutional forms and ideological obsessions which go far in the explanation of the worst political phenomena of our century – indeed of all time.

Primary and secondary education are at least as important as the higher sector in the overall process. The absence of easy exit for parents – their inability to take their children swiftly away from schools with which they are dissatisfied – has been crucial in the generation of low cognitive standards and tendentious ideology alike. In other words lack of exit connects with both malfunctions and dysfunctions in education. Sometimes parents may care deeply about children's low standards in reading and arithmetic. They may be shocked at the hostility to competition the school manifests. They may be deeply offended that the children call teachers 'Bill' or 'Mary' and that the school seems obsessed with issues of race and 'gender'. They may not, however, have the financial resources to move their children and they may not have enough confidence to complain. For these reasons inferior teaching and intellectual error can persist for decades. Parents who want to take their children out need either financial resources or strong and persistent characters allied to sound knowledge of the system.

What about the children of parents who care rather little or nothing about either literacy and numeracy or fundamental morality? Such parents will bring little or no pressure to bear on bad schools. A proper curriculum will be even less in evidence for their children. These will be protected in some degree, however, if parents who do care can exit the system. Thus, overall, the absence of competition and easy exit will affect the whole intake. Discernible here is an *a priori* description of the demand for compulsory schooling, to the effect that under public finance the demand for education tends to be insensitive and relatively powerless during the years of compulsory attendance.[175]

We can contrast this with the supply picture. The experts who control teacher education and the inspection and quality control services have decided that older generations of teachers

---

175 The notion of voluntary education is a bridge too far for present stomachs; but the arguments for compulsion are not properly explored, let alone well grounded.

and academics were wrong about education. Education is not the disinterested pursuit of knowledge or the search for moral goodness, which conceptions are crucial to the notion of reproducing our civilisation.[176] No, education is about equality and power, about pleasure and relaxation, about finding space for oneself, about self-esteem. Thus the curriculum must focus on the autonomy of childhood, the primacy of sex relations or race relations and the claims of rival culture. These ideas, gummed together with brutal insouciance, are the agenda of modern socialist education. Those who push them from the supply side run very little risk thereby. Certainly their own resources are not on the line.

By definition PC relies very heavily on public funds, because education in general does. Coulson is damning in his account of the failure of our publicly financed primary and secondary education. He notes that, historically, most successful education has always been private.[177] In any event, on both sides of the Atlantic, higher education is predominantly a creature of public monies, resting on a primary and secondary structure even more dependent on the state.

In fact, to repeat a point that can scarcely be stressed too much, private universities in the USA get huge public subventions, in different forms.[178] In any case, in both our countries many students arrive at university very badly prepared for higher education, via the normal route of preparation in state primary and secondary schools. Most people's educational profile is mainly formed within the milieu of public funds, whatever type of university they end up in.

The blurring of economic agency

Economic decision-making under socialism is blurred and uncertain. The conceptual, functional difference between supply and demand at times breaks down somewhat in the conditions of subsidised production. Given public finance and its circuitous pathways the suppliers are not literally selling and the demanders are not literally paying, or only in much disguised and therefore distorted terms.

---

176 Richard S. Peters *Ethics and Education*. Allen and Unwin, 1966; John White *The Aims of Education Restated*. Routledge and Kegan Paul, 1982.
177 Coulson *op. cit.*
178 Casse and Manno *op. cit.*, pp. 42–44.

Our intellectual culture has been dumbed down by this separation from market clarities. The American and British governments seem, moreover, to think nothing wrong with forking out huge sums to repair the disasters of pre-university schooling. Why should people in higher education have to be taught study skills? The economic term and the common sense name for such repetition are the same: waste. Rectifications are needed; but they should not be, or not routinely.

The gross underpreparedness of young people entering higher education is the core of the case put by Allan Bloom.[179] The case about schools is put even more bluntly by E. D. Hirsch, though the latter is contradictorily sanguine about American higher education.[180] I would simply ask: if school standards are so bad, how can universities be so good? And sick the schools certainly are.

Radical pathogens and conservative antibodies

On this pathological foundation extremist ideologies can be erected. What else but 'extremist' fits those 'educators' who say all men are rapists or all white people irretrievably evil? Could we conceivably have got to this if our nineteenth-century predecessors had not entrusted education to the state and the public purse? It is now clear that neo-Marxist theory got its account exactly the wrong way round. It is socialist education which depends on a healthy market for its *matériel* and its tax base. The neo-Marxists sang in unison that capitalism would collapse without the anaesthetising effects of education. In truth our education is a parasite of the free economy.

Against the excesses and deficits of socialist educational production what Scruton calls 'conservative antibodies' are not fully effective.[181] Their origin is the civil order and their operation integral to the working of a market economy. They do work to some extent in education. A plan by the Local Education Authority in one of the big London boroughs a few years ago to have the schools teach that homosexuality is as normal as heterosexual love was thwarted by massive opposition from

---

179 Bloom *op. cit.*
180 Hirsch *The Schools We Need: And Why We Don't Have Them, op. cit.*
181 Scruton 'Opening Fire in the Real Culture Wars' *op cit.*

Catholics, Moslems, Hindus, Sikhs etc. Indeed, in Britain the idea of promoting homosexuality via school has been put on the retreat across the whole country in the last few years. Perhaps this ancient moral taboo is one where public opinion can be mobilised. The standard advantage public choice theory has detected for unrepresentative opinion works only when the majority against an anomaly is mild, allowing the intense minority to get away with it. When the majority cares a lot, as it does about homosexualist indoctrination, the minority advantage melts away. Unfortunately the majority has not been so stirred to date *vis-à-vis* illiteracy and innumeracy, etc. There the minority have retained their advantage.

The key point then is that in many instances ideological infections are often insufficiently repelled; many germs get through. This partial vulnerability is akin to the system's failure fully to identify shortages and gluts of different outputs and eliminate them expeditiously. We suffer both from the general inefficient allocation of resources typical of public finance *and* from the special version of this which arises when the standard registration of the moral consensus is impeded. Wrong mathematics, wrong English, wrong reading schemes, wrong morals: all these and many more ideological pathogens have got through the defences.

The range of dangerous germs is now very considerable. Take the mistakes caused by people's confusing inalienable with contingent and consensually negotiated rights. Lots of people believe they have clear rights of access to other people's talents and work. The welfare state pumps out such ideas relentlessly. They are now of plague-like proportions. 'Rights' to such services are in fact purely conventional – dependent on our level of affluence and our degree of procedural consensus. We see this error dramatically exemplified in the recent expansion of British higher education. Lots of people fully expected this to be entirely funded by the state and government attempts to get consumers to bear some of the cost cause outrage.

Habituation to perverse ideas

Also significant for the operation of education's strange economy is the way in which our publics seem prepared to accept much of the corrupting praxis which in its distilled form becomes PC, as a price for the survival of welfare and other public services. To excise nonsense about green politics and animal rights, and PC along with it, we would have to clamp down on the schools the state provides, for example, and it provides the primary and secondary ones free at the point of use and the tertiary ones at the very least heavily subsidised. The public may well reject ideological nonsense in the schools. Its feeling that schools should be provided free at the point of use is far stronger.

Mr and Mrs Jones may disapprove of welfare scroungers and long-term welfare habituation. They may condemn the multiplication of 'rights' having no matching obligations. Nevertheless, there is always the possibility that one day the Jones family, too, might need those welfare payments. In a way, public tolerance of what it does not believe right and proper is a kind of prudential tacking. It is a signal to conservatives not to rock the boat too much. In recent decades such ambivalence has haunted many of the conservative attempts at reform in America and Britain.

Frum thinks Americans less conservative than is helpful to full-blown conservative policies, i.e. to a serious fiscal counter-reformation.[182] The truth is perhaps more subtle. Most citizens would probably like to see their whole society purged of its nonsense. This, though, is rather like being in favour of virtue or for the abolition of the common cold. Lots of people do not like the price tag on reforming public activities. The American and British publics, though mostly far from socialist, let alone PC, nevertheless want a whole range of public services pretty well left as they are for fiscal purposes.

The trouble, even duplicity, is that the public demand services they do not want to pay for. Taxation is what should fall on others. Many people seem blind to the fact that all taxpayers, one way or another, pay for such services. We are back to that sturdy support of residual socialism: fiscal illusion. Something seems free because our paying for it is remote and circuitous. This induces a paralysis in decision-making which suits extremism's books just fine. Nor is the circumstance strange, merely a case of old-fashioned human inertia and ambiguity.

---

182 Frum *op. cit.*, p. 31.

Habit, error and moral cowardice

There is widespread support, both popular and intellectual, for the public finance of education. Decades of heavy taxation have persuaded large numbers of people that those with higher earnings than they should be very heavily taxed to support their interests. There is also support for what Gerard Radnitzky calls 'churning' – the moving around of the funds of an increasingly middle class society.[183] The strong *prima facie* case that the former practice is conceptually quite close to theft and the latter deeply irrational seems to have escaped public attention.

Many individuals in the free societies have taken on board various attitudes objectively against the interests of most people. We can become habituated to error. Admittedly, the 'rational economy' is an ideal typical conceit. There will always be elements of irrationality in economic life, if only because life in general does not reduce to things economic. Even so, we need the ideal typical notion as a marker. There must be some point at which compounded economic irrationality will erode our civilisation. We certainly cannot afford it to dominate our educational arrangements. Private enterprise should be a much stronger presence in education, a development which would be massively in most people's interest. Yet millions seem to assume that the state can make a better go of our schools than the market would. Persuading the American and British public otherwise may prove a very difficult task.

Cowardice and fanaticism come into it too. In the media and in publishing, views unwelcome to their personnel are often excluded, even where this is economically irrational. PC enthusiasts call openly for censorship. Thus arises the madness that writers like Geoff Dench have had to hunt out those rare companies willing to publish their books. Dench for a long time found no one to take on his brilliant attack on feminism.[184] Sometimes people would like to break the PC ranks but are scared to. Some souls, to their shame and our sorrow, are habituated to moral cowardice. We should recall the way Solzhenitsyn took on the

183 Gerard Radnitzky 'Sorting Social Systems' in Gerard Radnitzky (ed.) *Values and the Social Order* Volume 3: *Voluntary Versus Coercive Orders.* Avebury, 1997, pp. 17–75.
184 Dench *op. cit.*

KGB and then ourselves send their weak western counterparts packing.

The corrupted humanist academe

The rise of a corrupted humanist academe is the worst example of producer-capture in the free societies. Public finance of education was always a disaster waiting to happen. Melanie Phillips has shown how subversion was present in modern British education long before the 1960s,[185] paving the way for an ascendancy. E. D. Hirsch finds the fatal years in America back in the 1920s in the Columbia University Teachers' College.[186] A glance at the secondary school curriculum pursued by Milton Friedman as a boy, however, suggests that the rot did not take wide effect in the first half of the century.[187]

In both countries the socialist praxis proceeded slowly for three-quarters of a century following state usurpation. There were obviously changes inherent in the state takeover, stronger in the American than in the British case. Coulson shows that managerialism and statism were strong in America from the mid-nineteenth century. Horace Mann was a supporter of look-and-say reading and by the beginning of the twentieth century phonetically based teaching of reading came under devastating attack in American schools.[188]

This disaster took longer to take root in Britain. Whenever egalitarian ideology or scientism are embedded in public services, however, they supply the auxiliary elements needed to push an intrinsically inefficient system into a disastrous socialist posture. Until the 1960s education was spared the more virulent forms of egalitarian doctrine. Even so, the incorporation of education by the state both in America and in Britain must from the first have compromised economic efficiency. In America, the all-ability high school, a quintessentially socialist arrangement, came half a century earlier than it did in Britain. On the other hand child-centred pedagogy, another wrong departure, seems to have established itself far more strongly in Britain.

---

185 Melanie Phillips *All Must Have Prizes*. Little, Brown, 1996, pp. 119–206.
186 Hirsch *The Schools We Need: And Why We Don't Have Them op. cit.*, Chapter 4.
187 Friedman *op. cit.*
188 Coulson *op. cit.* pp. 160–168.

One thing is clear. The persistence or displacement of an educational practice depends on the views of the élite. Once these shift significantly, practices can change rapidly. Until a few decades ago, the American and British élites mostly held a view of education and public morals much the same as that of the majoritarian consensus. It is when the élite embrace radicalism that the worst damage occurs. In the 1960s a 'wayward élite' arose, promoting educational arrangements quite different from what a free market could conceivably generate.[189] Such is the pseudo-libertarian dispensation represented at its worst by PC. Our corrupted humanism is 'pseudo-libertarian' because although it is as free-wheeling imaginatively as libertarianism, it lacks the disciplinary fiscal constraints proposed by genuine libertarians.

We have long known that the main internal threat to civilisation comes from certain ideologues, mostly in the education system, above all the universities, the latter's ideological postures facilitated and prefigured by the primary and secondary schools. What has slipped scholarly attention has been the strange calculus on which such postures depend, one in which public funds displace or subsidise private ones.

Public finance changes the principles of production

The notion of free enterprise education is crucial for counterfactual reflection; indeed, it is quite odd that the free societies do not realise the historical normality of private education, institutional socialism having become only in modern times the norm.[190]

Education in the free societies is one of a number of instances – welfare administration is another – where as a result of public finance a vast flow of resources has been put to uses radically different from those which would arise privately. For one thing the volume of resources is almost certainly more under public finance than it would be privately. This does not necessarily mean effective demand would be smaller under private finance. It does mean that resources are less efficiently used.

Let us, casting aside Utopianism, assume that all economies are liable to waste. This leaves us with two desirable economic

---

189 O'Keeffe *The Wayward Elite op. cit.*
190 Coulson *op. cit.* Part II.

categories – investment and consumption – and one, waste, which we must strive to eliminate. History offers two principal ways of seeking this outcome: capitalism and socialism, the *leitmotifs* of this book. In truth there is no contest. Capitalism gives you more investment, more consumption and less waste than socialism does. In a mainly market economy, however, socialisation of any activity suitable for private production, adversely reorders the principles regulating output. In the educational case, the curriculum, pedagogy and evaluation will be different from those a free market would engender. There will be a different subject-mix, different teaching styles and examinations and different authority relations. Above all, patterns of investment, consumption and waste will be very different.

From the nineteenth-century beginnings of compulsion and public finance, and especially since the 1960s, American and British education has featured increased consumption, diminished investment and rampant waste, compared to the pattern which spontaneous market evolution would have secured. Only free market education will yield an efficient balance between consumption and investment, one expressing citizens' preferences under conditions of risk bearing directly on decision-makers. If having read antinomian propaganda qualifies you as a social worker, you may choose this path. If there are no such outlets you may face more demanding imperatives. You might choose engineering, a subject with a vast corpus of achievement, thus far in our free society largely impervious to ideological corruption. Who knows if sociology or English literature will ever be able to claim a comparably uncontaminated status again?

Western socialist education generates too much (subsidised) consumption, whereas Communist education, whatever its achievements in literacy, numeracy and scientific knowledge, was inevitably part of the Communist chaos, an *anti-economy* inevitably frustrating genuine investment and consumption alike, with its bleak 'decades of insolent plans, haste and waste' as Landes says.[191]

---

191 David Landes *The Wealth and Poverty of Nations*. Little, Brown, 1998, p. 497.

Socialist education in market and socialist societies

Socialist education in a free society thus differs significantly from education under full socialism. In America and Britain education is controlled by an élite, loosely united ideologically, for whom education is their main power-base, though they are also strong in the welfare state and have some support in the media, publishing and show business. Communist education was controlled by an élite with society-wide power. The curricular implications of this difference are dramatic.

Communism had an 'investment' curriculum, chiming with the Marxist emphasis on physical capital formation.[192] Whether, once the Marxist patina had been scraped off, this was a decent curriculum, is a subject beyond our terms of reference.[193] Communist investment, however, was generally unchecked by market utility. The curriculum, like everything else, was assimilated to the Communist waste system.

This contrasts with a hypothetical free enterprise curriculum where the ratio of investment (for further learning and careers) to consumption (for present utility) is left to the market. With the advent of public finance and compulsory attendance such a dispensation has become largely hypothetical, the reality in free societies being control of a socialist system by its own internal élite. In principle, though, this dispensation is the only proper and efficient basis for the curriculum.

There is shocking waste in American and British education, given poor English and mathematics teaching, direct products of 'progressive' ideology. Illiteracy and innumeracy mean waste. The overall effectiveness of the curriculum is much reduced as large numbers of pupils, unable to read or number properly, are excluded from either effective investment or consumption decisions. Much of the curriculum must be impenetrable for many of them. All societies face the problem that the curriculum is more intelligible to children from educated than to those from less educated families. The progressive intelligentsia have deliberately compounded this problem. In many cases it will be

---

192 David Lane *Politics and Society in the USSR*. Martin Robertson, 1978, p. 494.

193 Polish sociologists have repeatedly told me that because Communism was a corrupt system its educational arrangements were correspondingly corrupt.

only those children who share the culture of that intelligentsia who will understand what the curriculum signifies.

Curriculum and the discovery process under public finance

Kirzner and other Austrian economists have spoken of the discovery process which permits the entrepreneur to make profits by exploiting gaps in production and discrepancies in price.[194] The Austrian view is that so far from entailing perfect markets, free enterprise is required because there is no such thing as a perfect market. Society is characterised by massive gaps in knowledge of prices and preferences. Economic agents will seek to discover what is scarce and profitable. Innovation is the process of moving scarce resources into profitable uses. How does this apply to education?

Curriculum innovation is a discovery process in which competing interest groups of intellectual/ideological convictions strive for scarce resources and status within schools and other educational institutions. Ivor Goodson has written eloquently on this.[195] It is clear that the possibilities of advantageous discovery and innovation remain in our public sectors. In such a context, however, they are *distorted by public finance*. Their costs are heavily socialised and their benefits to innovators much enhanced by the reduction of risk which public finance effects. Once these risks are socialised in this way, informed supply often becomes cosseted and privileged. Unrepresentative material gets bedded in and the curriculum becomes increasingly remote from standard preferences and preoccupations.

Nor is it only the supply side calculus which is distorted. The sense of scarcity is anaesthetised on the demand side too. Once the risks of failure are socialised informed demand often becomes a kind of ideological insider trading. Education today has partly fractured the moral consensus of earlier modernity by partially suborning supply and demand. In addition, antinomian ideologies are credentialised by the growth of corresponding, often public sectoral, outlets. More people are drawn into the study of soft social science and ideologised humanities than would be if

---

194 Israel M. Kirzner *How Markets Work: Disequilibrium, Entrepreneurship and Discovery*, Hobart Paper No. 133. Institute for Economic Affairs, 1997.
195 Ivor Goodson *School Subjects and Curriculum Change*. Croom Helm, 1983.

they had to pay all the bill. Fewer pursue the more demanding pathways of science and technology.

On socialist educational entrepreneurship

Public choice theory has shown the subversion which arises in state bodies when economic decisions are mediated through a political structure. This distorts the patterns of costs and benefits, changing the calculus of decision-makers. Precisely this insight needs to be used for analysing the educational arrangements of the free societies.

The defining characteristic activity of market economies – entrepreneurship – is present in these arrangements, but in caricatural form. There are curricular and pedagogic innovators, even salesmen, of a sort, but in a mocking mimicry of real market activity. The difference concerns the pattern of risk. Educational entrepreneurs may risk their reputations on this or that new idea; but they will not typically be risking their own financial resources.

The managerial élite of education are allowed extraordinary freedom in their quest to manage other people's minds. Such freedom springs from the tradition whereby élites are regarded as competent. It goes back to the years when educational leadership and the public were rightly assumed to share a common view of the purposes of education. The fact that this unity no longer holds is partly disguised by the lack of easy exit for dissatisfied consumers. This means that educational malfunctions and dysfunctions go uncorrected, sometimes for decades.

Frum asks how long university students would study Foucault if they had to meet all the bill.[196] Coulson asks how long the wrong teaching of reading would survive in a privately financed dispensation.[197] Similarly, we may speculate how long privately financed schools would persist without rote learning of multiplication tables. The decades-long refusal by our educational élites to insist on phonics-based reading and the rote learning of tables are quintessential socialist perversity, with dysfunctional consequences, somewhat akin to the old Soviet insistence on wrong drilling bits in their oil-extraction technology. As for the 'real books' fantasy, the notion that children

---

196 Frum *op. cit.*, p. 28.
197 Coulson *op.cit.*, pp 367–368.

will learn just by being surrounded by books, it is a veritable pedagogic Lysenkoism. Who would pay cash on the nail for children to be taught under such assumptions? Only when fiscal illusion has sufficiently blunted the rigour and sensitivity of demand and supply, are such anomalies possible. PC is simply the latest and most offensive of these anomalies.

What sociology of knowledge should properly have pursued

The neo-Marxists thought our educational problems were all about capitalism. On the contrary, they are mostly functions of socialism. Our education has long been wayward. Scholarship has not got to grips properly with our destructive instructional mode, which has institutionalised inferior substitutes for our traditional preoccupations. In particular, the élite have sought to replace the basic issues of knowledge and morality with the second-order concerns of power and equality. The result is confusion, a deep-seated cognitive and moral chaos. Subsidised educational entrepreneurship, where success and failure are not properly monitored, has led to partial corrosion both of the market and of the civil order.

Many educational entrepreneurs have indeed waxed wealthy on the basis of failure. Wrong theories of reading, wrong theories of morality, wrong theories of mathematics: all these and many more have been established and preserved. True, whether these theories are right or wrong, the wealth of educational entrepreneurs will not usually be on an exemplary bourgeois scale. The Bill Gates of the curriculum seems an improbable being. But very valuable rents – comprising power, prestige and income – are available, and beyond these, in exceptional cases, the lecture circuit, journalism, writing and publishing, can make some such subsidised entrepreneurs rich in more purely capitalist terms too. The names of some of these rich socialist/capitalist educational entrepreneurs (SCEEs) are obvious. The difference between them and genuine capitalists is that there is no proper market to test out their successes and failures.

There is a private market for education books and other *matériel*; but it is massively constrained by the demands made on it by the public sector. Thousands of sociologists whose incomes come mainly from the state decide that Foucault was a valuable thinker and hundreds of thousands of students are thereby constrained to read him, with predictable effects on

91

private publishing houses. Capitalism is involved; but only because the matter has been established by the public purse.

While these curricular entrepreneurs are making their way, they are usually employed in publicly financed or at least heavily subsidised universities. This is where and when they most exploit their subsidised situation. There are risks to reputation in their activities even in this cossetted state; but these are small beer compared to putting one's own fortune on the line. In any case, a majority of educational rent-seekers never step outside this cosy condition, never get beyond the rewards internal to the public sector.

Why does this matter? Because whatever differences in success there may be, it is inevitable that subsidised entrepreneurship will yield different curricular and pedagogic outcomes from entrepreneurship under personal liability. We have a socialist, state-subsidised curriculum. What do curricular entrepreneurs and welfare dependants have in common? It is that in both cases the provision of public funds permits the simultaneous privatisation of activities and the socialisation of their consequences. Crash courses in literacy etc. will be provided – by taxpayers – for the student who has gone through school with his potential negated by the application of wrong theory after wrong theory. These theories will have enriched the people who inspired his neglect, and provided many of their followers with income and employment. Sometimes there are not even antidote courses, society merely absorbing the negative outcomes, and socialising the ill effects with handouts to unemployables.

The temptations of ghostly resources

To move away from the market in matters economic is to distance oneself from reality. The economic reality of the human condition is perpetual scarcity, even in the most affluent societies, and thus the need for the most realistic weighing of costs and benefits. Socialists love spending other people's money. Populations by contrast, are tax-averse. When socialist mischief works in the gap between the public's desire for services and their extreme reluctance to pay for them, it can operate on deficit finance. America and Britain till recently paid for their habituation to 'public' services by running up public debt. The spending of non-existent money, belonging to no one, is the most seductive corruption of all. In such circumstances the distinction between supply and demand partly breaks down as an irresponsible élite alienated from mainstream opinion reproduces itself. Why should such shadowy funds not be used irresponsibly? They owe their tenuous existence to irresponsibility. PC is the worst modern outcome to date of a fiscal carelessness so established it is almost endemic, and a warning that freedom is truly about discipline, not licence.

Socialist education and the problem of educability

In the American and British case, the reality is not a consumer-focused curriculum for everyone. Success is as always easier for those from educated families. The worst misuse of resources will be in badly taught English and mathematics, where adverse effects will occur across the board, for all social groups and levels of intelligence. Where the higher education curriculum is least corrupted ideologically, e.g. in science, technology and medicine, the corresponding pathways in prior education will be least compromised. The worst ideological clutter in primary and secondary schools will surround curricular prerequisites for humanities and social science. In other words it is the teaching of history, literature, elementary sociology and morality which most prefigure the PC aspects of the university world.

The millions of people in our societies who have studied social science, social administration and humanities at the tertiary level, constitute, with their children, the main PC constituency. The free ride, the subsidised consumption spree, across the whole educational span, is mostly for these self-selecting legions. Those who teach the pop-sentimentality curriculum in schools, or the obfuscating Post-Modernist one in universities, are a sizeable section of the new middle classes. The preoccupations of this group are nominally open to all, but the many people who do not share them must find themselves and their children in varying degree excluded.

This bears hugely on the question of educability. If the risks inherent in the use of all scarce resources were more apparent in education, and bore more obviously on teachers and students, the bizarre new curriculum of recent decades could not long survive. At present, though the bulk of the funds facilitating education are public, there is a strange process of intra-curricular privatisation going on, whereby a powerful élite effectively restricts the use of a sizeable stream of scarce resources to those party to its strange ideological fancies.

There is no conspiracy involved. The movers and shakers of PC believe their own propaganda in all probability, though PC, like every powerful ideology, will also attract its share of main-chancers and opportunists. By definition the grip these PC ideas have in the educational lives of the free societies is a disaster. That said, the curriculum probably still works for more people than it fails. As was noted before, there would be mass rebellion if this were not so. As it happens, the British evidence is quite strong that most schoolchildren approve of its secondary school version.[198] Even so, many people, including many working-class children, would better appreciate a more straight-forward instrumental curriculum in which risks were more obvious and potential payoffs clearer. The public finance of education obfuscates educational decision-making by socialising risks and establishing perverse pathways through the whole educational experience. The ideological blockage that operates in parts of higher education, effectively screening the students *vis-à-vis* a prescribed conformity, and reinforced by a perversely preserved inadequate teaching of core skills, reaches back down to the lower stages of education.

The fatal assumption of competence and benevolence

The substantive content of the curriculum and the forms of teaching employed, as well as the methods of assessment, in countries like America and Britain, still reflect, though today undeservedly, the belief in practitioner competence, autonomy and benevolence which PC and other cults have so gravely abused. Effectively, senior practitioners have had a free hand. In addition to the high regard of the public, the élite have also had access to their resources. This was always far from optimal economically, but did not much offend morally or intellectually as long as such leadership had more or less the same views as the rest of society. It may be doubted whether a return to curricular sanity can be effected without drastic changes. The last (short) chapter will consider what might be done.

---

198 D. J. O'Keeffe *Truancy in English Secondary Schools.* HMSO, 1994, pp. 70–74.

5 | Conclusions and proposals

Introduction

The *general relationship* between public finance and intellectual corruption is beyond doubt highly adverse. We can properly appeal to extreme examples to summon up this general case. We need not, indeed *should* not, in considering the links between finance and moral and intellectual integrity, confine our thoughts to such favoured societies as the United States and Great Britain. Communism provides a vast evidence on the debased intellectual results of excessive reliance on public finance. The Nazi slave state, too, was in the main a phenomenon of public finance. The Nazi story shows that even when the private economy remains relatively active, **hypertrophy** of the state and the consequent access of unaccountable ideologues to public funds, constitute an extreme danger to political and intellectual sanity, decency and the security of individuals and groups. The modern totalitarian dictators have surpassed the worst tyrants of old and they have paid their way in public funds.

PC: a totalitarianism for tiny tots

True, it seems highly improbable that PC in America or Britain will ever operate on a scale to match such ills as these. Thus far PC has generated lots of hatred but not murder. Consequently, as we noted in Chapter 2, some people think it pointlessly portentous to compare PC with such unfathomable despotisms.[199] In fact such comparison is not portentous but enlightening. No one is going to say that PC creates evil on a similar scale to that of the Communists or Nazis. It is the *ideological likenesses* which so compellingly stand comparison. Indeed, the family similarities are striking. PC is a mutating socialist praxis with its roots

---

199 McGowan *op. cit.*

95

in a relativism inherited precisely from the Marxist tradition. PC shares in the extremism, the hostility to the real world, the implacable resentments, the paranoia and the ideological instability which mark totalitarianism proper. It is undeveloped politically only because its leading members play the very dangerous game of trying to keep it undeveloped, a kind of totalitarianism for tiny tots.

Like the real article PC corrupts words and meanings. Like more fully fledged totalitarianism it institutionalises the adulation of odious individuals and charlatans, persecutes decent people and demands ideological conformity where it can. Furthermore, some of its separatist manifestations are uncomfortably, eerily like the ascriptive reasonings and practices made forever infamous by the Nazis.

Why we should resist PC

We should resist PC on the grounds both of its intrinsic character and of the consequences which could follow if it were ever to achieve a wider institutionalisation. It is self-evidently wrong to promote hatred and division between people on the grounds of race or sex or culture. This is precisely what PC has led to, whatever the egalitarian campaigns may once have intended. As to what would follow were PC to gain a wider following or a deeper grip, we do not know. Maybe socialist intellectuals think they can control their ideological Frankenstein. Amongst the shrewdest of them there is honest anxiety on this score.[200] There is every reason to think, in fact, that the results of an expansion of PC would be terrible, and in particular, that PC might pave the way for some other as yet unknown horror. Certainly PC has benefitted from a slumber of reason in American and British life, precisely where these two societies should maintain the liveliest defence of freedom: in their education systems.

All this is to claim no more than that public finance in the free societies, indisputably connected to such ills as mass illiteracy and innumeracy, also connects with phenomena of totalitarian tendency. This is not at all to say that some kind of reborn Stalinism or Hitlerism will inevitably inherit the free world. Indeed, it is also abundantly clear that many publicly financed

---

200 Hall *op. cit.*

activities in the free societies cannot by any stretch of the imagination be termed 'corrupt'. Many are innocent, involving good intentions on the part of those involved. Actually, it is quite probable that a *majority* are inoffensive or even benevolent in their intentions. Rather fewer, we may be sure, given our knowledge of politically administered as opposed to market-based economic activity, have favourable *outcomes*. All the same, in the educational case, a majority of our populations are literate, numerate and decent, notwithstanding their getting most of their education on the basis of public funds. Does this mean we should foreswear condemnatory words like 'corruption'? Is this a hyperbole to be struck out along with portentous comparisons?

No, it is not. Though most people can read, write and number, and are law-abiding, and though most lead at least reasonably affluent lives in our kind of society, there are enough alarming things to supply an indictment of our educational arrangements. It is all a question of emphasis. In America and Britain a majority can cope in terms of the mechanics of life in an advanced society, though the range of competence is naturally enormous and there is a worryingly large group who though not illiterate or innumerate are nevertheless rather poorly educated. A very large minority, however, cannot cope at all. That is the problem. Moreover – to reiterate the central argument of this book – we should not think only of the *current* ills of universities where free speech is prevented and exotic hatreds flourish, or of mass ignorance. We must also consider – as this book has done – the *background* to PC, the long line of increasingly exotic egalitarian variants and the persistently bitter campaigns against the family and the school as traditionally understood.

Every canon of tradition and culture has one by one been attacked. Teachers and parents – indeed society as a whole – have lost out in the assault deliberately mounted by departments of sociology and of humanities, colleges of education and certain primary and secondary schools, against adult authority.

This attack, which has gone on for decades, is the origin of the partial moral erosion of our society, an erosion which has impeded proper learning. This moral decay is of critical significance. It seems inconceivable that private finance would have facilitated it so readily, inconceivable also that without such cumulative moral and intellectual destruction anything so monstrous as PC could have gained a grip.

Some results of educational socialism

The minorities adversely affected by educational socialism number many millions. We can scarcely be smug about competent majorities when we have so many people who are *incompetent*. Millions of people are illiterate and innumerate and many millions more are ill-educated, morally as well as culturally. These faults result from a corrupt anticulture having established itself in our educational arrangements. Many people live in poverty mainly because they learned so little in school. Others, including some affluent ones, are immoral because school – among other moral agencies – gave them no proper moral bearings or displaced those they had. If such outcomes are not to be called 'corruption' then it is hard to see what might be.

The very least charge we can lay against the way education has been organised is that in many cases it has not provided a sound moral and intellectual formation. True, it is apparent that millions have risen socially through school and college. Without doubt education has been the major pathway to an increasingly middle-class society. The case against *socialist* education is that but for its ideological obsessions the process of middle-class enlargement would have gone even further. Education has interrupted, modified, made smaller, the spontaneous, unplanned, upward social convergence of the masses which characterises late capitalism. You can be as clever as you like; but if you are from an uneducated background, and you also have the misfortune to attend a poor school, trying to get on academically is like climbing a steep hill when you are carrying heavy luggage.

Millions more should have opted into the middle-class dispensation but, sadly, have been trapped. What they learned at school did not suffice to break the chains of deprivation which bind a shamefully large impoverished minority. These shortcomings could not have occurred if there were not, both in America and Britain, powerful élites actively hostile to our civilisation, élites which seek to disseminate antinomian beliefs and lifestyles among the population. Their success can be measured by the fact that what should have been a small *lumpenproletariat* by now has become a very big welfariat. A significant minority now lives on the state.

Socialist ideologies have partially eroded
the moral order

Destructive theories have flourished in education, as sane and reasonable beliefs have come under attack. Some of these theories are moral and ideological, others technical. The former make up the deadly egalitarian afflatus. The latter include provenly wrong ideas on the teaching of reading and introductory mathematics. It may well be sinking in now that all children need instruction in synthetic phonics if they are to read to their best potential and that multiplication tables must be learned by heart if people are to be at all proficient mathematically; but the American and British élites are proving remarkably obdurate in defence of their errors. In any case, it is the moral theories informing the progressive educational praxis which are most destructive. Even the very best of technical theories *vis-à-vis* the learning of reading and mathematics and the most lavish finance will not work adequately if the children do not see the moral imperatives of learning.[201]

This book has tried to explain how our peculiar Western version of socialist education connects over many decades with inadequacies in basic cognitive skills, and with cultural, intellectual and moral shortcomings. Publicly financed schooling has been at least a necessary condition of these outcomes. Students have been taught to disdain facts but also to be dismissive of old-established ideas and conventions and credulous in the face of new ones. In the absence of such educational deficits, an incoherent and destructive phenomenon like PC would not have been able to take shape. It is entirely proper, then, that we be wary of public finance and the state. Indeed, the havoc created by socialist education deserves more complaint and contempt than it has generated. State education is more favourably regarded by the electorates and publics in our countries than it deserves to be. PC and its related and background excesses flourish not because the American and British peoples are PC but because they do not want to disturb the financial arrangements of education. They have become habituated to inferior schooling. They would not tolerate comparable inefficiency for five minutes when they buy their cars or groceries.

---

201 O'Keeffe *op. cit.*

Thus the future of education will be a difficult one whether we act or not. If we do not, the rot will continue. If we do, our enemies will fight us all the way. Let us assume that battle is undertaken, though it is hard to see this happening full-bloodedly without a return to conservative government.

Determination and privatisation will be needed

Whenever the fight begins, how may all this confusion and malice be contained and – we hope – reversed? The battle will call for much determination on our part. It also seems very un-likely that the pathology could ever be definitively reversed with-out a major recourse to private finance. We have to create more competition among suppliers and greater opportunities for exit by consumers. Maybe James Tooley's new book, showing how much more willing many poorer countries are to use market forces in the co-ordination of their educational arrangements, will inspire conservative politics to better things.[202] If we want to stop things getting worse, and certainly if we entertain any hope that they might get better, we will need a radical change of mind and tack on the part of the conservative movements in our two countries. Sadly, it is not clear whether in America or Britain today there is sufficient stomach for the momentous battle it will take to displace socialist education in general and PC in particular. Certainly it is hard to see the Democrats in the USA or Labour in Britain giving any kind of a decent lead. They are themselves in good measure PC and they are philistine in their cultural beliefs and tastes. Let us assume, nevertheless, that the required nerve is available. How then shall we proceed?

On reversing socialist education

Socialism is a system for weakening the masses and making them prey to parasitic élites. Antony Flew was right in calling one of his books *Power to the Parents*.[203] Such power is, indeed, what we want. Only parental power is sufficiently strong, inter-ested and resolute to bring about high general educational stand-ards. Moreover, only parental power can fine-tune a curriculum, catering for differing needs, protecting genuine and academically

---

202 James Tooley *The Global Education Industry* Institute of Economic Affairs, 1999.
203 Flew *op. cit.*

sound minority interests, such as the classics, for example. Laurie Norcross has written on the effects of egalitarian envy and fanaticism on the teaching of classics.[204] It has been in our socialist education system that PC and related ideologies have flourished and that the study of Latin and Greek – and much else in the traditional curriculum – has withered. Markets protect not only the general but also the legitimate particular interest.

On the other hand Andrew Coulson has now established, seemingly incontrovertibly, that efficient and successful education, such as characterised ancient Athens or Medieval Islam, or nineteenth-century America and Britain before the advent of compulsion, has *always been private.* Only demand-led schooling can release and realise the dynamics of innovation.[205] The reason we want private education is that it will generate a richer and more varied as well as a more successfully delivered curriculum.

Private education works because parents have a vested interest both in their children and in the resources they commit to educating them. It should be stressed that Coulson favours profit-making schools. Profit-making private schools will work even better than non-profit-making ones because an educational bourgeoisie has a deep financial interest in securing the successful teaching of children. Such a bourgeoisie is by definition more pledged to success than any non-profit-making school, let alone than any rigid, bureaucratised state-school could be.

A brief word on the problem of compulsion

Compulsory education too is a crucial issue, one desperately in need of sustained examination. Milton and Rose Friedman rightly, and as long as twenty years ago, identified compulsion as at least a fellow-travelling socialist phenomenon.[206] This particular state-enhancing device has yet to be given its intellectual *coup de grâce,* however. We simply do not know enough about it. I am certain that it is a supplier-fortifying mechanism. Compulsion enhances the state and fortifies the suppliers because it transfers discretion from the public to the school.

---

204 Lawrence Norcross 'The Classics: Small Latin and Less Greek' in Dennis O'Keeffe (ed.) *The Wayward Curriculum.* Social Affairs Unit, 1986.
205 Coulson *op. cit.,* Chapter 9 'What Makes Schools Work?'
206 Friedman and Friedman *op. cit.,* Chapter 6.

If a student attends voluntarily (more usually if parents want their children to attend) suppliers have to attend to parental preferences. Compulsion much reduces this imperative. While this is enough to make us suspicious, we do not have the full measure of the thing yet. It needs a few good doctorates and some decent articles and books. When we know more and have explained compulsion more successfully, we will be in a position to decide whether school should be voluntary or compulsory and to what degree.

In matters of elimination, then, we can say so far that public finance has to be bit by bit ushered out, along with the Leninist conceit of planned and centralised curriculum, and that compulsory attendance needs to be properly probed and evaluated. Many substantive changes will happen spontaneously with the increasing marketisation of learning. Private schools will seek the best pedagogic methods and private research firms will work with them. Minorities may favour progressive pedagogies and a child-centred curriculum. In a free society, let them. For the most part, under competitive conditions their favoured approaches will not survive very long. They would not have appeared at all had the ordinary people been consulted in their capacity as intellectual decision-makers. When the continuous consultation of market forces occurs they will be much diminished.

Establishing an educational bourgeoisie

All those trends already favouring private education, education which is relatively free from state influence, should be encouraged. We already know that despite the public's educational habituation to public finance, there is great and growing support for private education. As economies grow richer there will continue to be a constant leakage away from the inferior products of state-provided schooling and into private education. Reforming governments should aim at reducing levels of taxation to facilitate this continuing process.

Examination boards, inspectoral services, and the ancillary cleaning and refectory services should be privatised – set on a commercial footing. Maybe we should consider for at least some decades paying all the salaries of teachers in private schools at some basic rate, which schools could then top up, a teachers' salary equivalent of the students' vouchers. This will clash with preferences for level playing fields in taxation policy but we need above all to establish a large bourgeois interest in education and such a subsidy does in some degree get round the problem that those who pay privately pay twice.

Until resources, risks and rewards are more closely linked the irresponsible management of the curriculum by a wayward élite will continue. People who cannot or will not teach literacy or numeracy or basic morals to our children should be properly exposed for the first time to parental preference, and indeed marketisation will soon do this, requiring them to change or redirecting them to schools catering for parents who subscribe to the progressive credo. A fair supposition is that such subscribers would soon prove to be a remarkably small minority. In the university world too, I would expect PC and Post-Modernism and the rest to survive, but on a much diminished basis.

We must avoid coercion and further bureaucratisation

What we must avoid is any further bureaucratisation. It is crucial that reform should avoid heavy-handed curricular prescription and proscription. We need a bias against *coercion*. PC, a mutation of 'progressivism', now demands a new coercion following the long progressive attack on standard morals. PC advocacy now calls for speech codes etc., which would kill intellectual pluralism. This coercion is precisely what a free society must resist, just as it should have prevented the partial dismantling of adult authority which has occurred. Coercion is the least effective mass-policy instrument in societies like ours, really appropriate only for criminal deviants.

If many university teachers have PC views the way to unseat them is through intellectual argument and the provision of competitive conditions. Within all public services there should be a maximum stress on competition. There should be as much devolution and decentralisation as possible. This will allow some odious views to continue; but bureaucratisation probably facilitates them even more. There is no sign in the British case, for example, that the National Curriculum has done anything to reverse socialist ideologies. The removing of monopoly powers in teacher education and other public services, by contrast, would in time allow alternative viewpoints to make themselves felt. Indeed, these monopoly powers could and should be removed even under a régime of public finance. In a free society attempts to eliminate ideological excesses by political administration are not likely to work and are against the spirit of freedom to boot.

The strong discipline education needs has to be sharply distinguished from coercion, since it aims at pupils/students coming to share in its moral and intellectual principles. Education is about the reproduction of our civilisation, the emergence of free adult beings. Parents and teachers have a right and duty to demand detailed moral conformity from children. At the same time different children clearly need different moral dispensations. The state is not capable of such finely tuned moral management, which is not its business anyway. For the governments in the free societies now to panic and to try to impose strong discipline on the population would be the opposite of their earlier error in encouraging the weakening of adult authority – but it would still be a grave error.

Obviously, the radical changes envisaged here cannot be made overnight. If we recognise that public finance will predominate for some years to come we must swallow our impatience and think as clearly as possible. The appropriate policy for the public sector of education, from the primary to the tertiary level, is as much variety and competition and flexibility as possible. In any case, the wait may not be all that long. The way information technology is progressing now, exit from an unsatisfactory educational experience is going to be more and more easily available.

Finally we must bear in mind that there are no Utopias, no perfect arrangements. The market economy, however, is vastly superior to any other way of managing scarce resources. A tragic misreading of education by our nineteenth-century forebears separated it for well over a century from the only system capable of organising and continuously correcting so vast an undertaking as the society-wide moral and intellectual instruction of the young. Future historians may come to believe that the worst mistake of modernity in the free societies was the entrusting of education to the vagaries of socialist organisation. It is time to bring learning and capitalism together again. This conjuncture will not be the end of corruption, intellectual or otherwise; but there are good grounds for thinking that intellectual perversity, including perversity of the PC kind, will have a much harder time of it, and that is surely a prospect worth working for.

Bibliography

Allen, W. B. 'The Fear of Disrepute' in Digby Anderson (ed.) *This Will Hurt*. Social Affairs Unit, London, 1995.

Althusser, Louis 'Ideology and Ideological State Apparatuses' in Ben Cosin (ed.) *Education, Structure and Society*. Penguin, Harmondsworth, 1972.

Apple, Michael W. *Education and Power*. Routledge and Kegan Paul, London, 1995.

Ashford, Nigel (reviewing Alan Charles Kors and Harvey Silvergate *The Shadow University: The Betrayal of Liberty on America's Campuses*. Free Press, 1998) *Free Life* 29 April 1999, pp. 7–8.

Bakunin, Michael *Statism and Anarchy*. Cambridge University Press, Cambridge, 1990.

Barcan, Alan 'English: Two Decades of Attrition' in Dennis O'Keeffe (ed.) *The Wayward Curriculum*. Social Affairs Unit, London, 1986.

Bernstein, Basil 'Class and Pedagogies: Visible and Invisible' in *Class, Codes and Control*, Vol. 3. Routledge and Kegan Paul, London, 1975.

Bernstein, Richard *Dictatorship of Virtue*. Knopf, New York, 1994.

Bloom, Allan *The Closing of the American Mind*. Simon and Schuster, New York, 1988.

Boghossian, Paul A. 'What the Sokal Hoax Ought to Teach Us'. *Times Literary Supplement,* 13 December 1996, pp. 14–15.

Bowles, Samuel and Gintis, Herbert *Schooling in Capitalist America*. Routledge and Kegan Paul, London, 1976.

Bowles, Samuel and Gintis, Herbert *Democracy and Capitalism: Property, Community and the Contradictions of Modernity,* Routledge and Kegan Paul, London, 1986.

Buchanan, J. M. *et al.* (eds) *Towards a Theory of Rent-Seeking Society.* Texas A&M University Press, College Station, TX, 1980.

Burkard, Tom *The End of Illiteracy: The Holy Grail of Clackmannanshire.* CPS, London, 1999.

Casse, Daniel and Manno, Bruno V. 'The Cost and Price of College and the Value of Higher Education.' *Academic Questions* 11(4), Fall 1998, pp. 42–44.

Chubb, John E. and Moe, Terry M. *Politics, Markets and America's Schools.* Brookings Institution, Washington, DC, 1990.

Cohn, Norman *The Pursuit of the Millennium: Revolutionary Millenarians and Mystical Anarchists of the Middle Ages.* Paladin, London, 1970.

Coldman, Colin and Shepherd, Ken 'Mathematics: The Campaign for "Real Maths" in Secondary Schools' in Dennis O'Keeffe *The Wayward Curriculum.* Social Affairs Unit, London, 1986.

Cooper, Bruce and O'Keeffe, Dennis 'Sweetness and Light in Schools: The Sentimentalisation of Children' in Digby Anderson and Peter Mullen (eds.) *Faking It: The Sentimentalisation of Modern Society.* Penguin, London, 1998.

Cooper, Bruce and Speakman, Sheree T *Optimizing Educational Resources.* JAI Press, 1996.

Coulson, Andrew J. *Market Education: The Unknown History.* Transaction, New Brunswick, NJ, 1999.

Danziger, Sheldon 'Overview' in Special Issue, 'Defining and Measuring the Underclass', *Focus* 12(1) Spring/summer 1989, Institute for Research on Poverty, University of Wisconsin, Madison.

Dench, Geoff *Transforming Men: Changing Patterns of Dependency and Dominance in Gender Relations.* Transaction, New Brunswick, NJ, 1996.

D'Souza, Dinesh *Illiberal Education.* Free Press, New York, 1991.

Ferrera, Cornelia 'Isis and the Crisis of Morality' in Christine M. Kelly (ed.) *The Enemy Within: Radical Feminism in the Christian Churches*. Family Publications, Milton Keynes, 1992.

Finn, Chester E. Jr 'Can Our Colleges Fix our Schools?' *Academic Questions,* Spring 1991.

Finn, Chester E. Jr 'Giving it Away.' *Salisbury Review,* Summer 1998.

Fish, Stanley *Professional Correctness: Literary Studies and Political Change*. Clarendon Press, Oxford, 1995.

Flew, Antony *Power to the Parents: Reversing Educational Decline*. Sherwood, London, 1987, pp. 93–111.

Friedman, Milton *Capitalism and Freedom*. University of Chicago Press, Chicago, 1962.

Friedman, Milton and Friedman, Rose *Free to Choose*. Secker and Warburg, London, 1980.

Frum, David 'It's Big Government Stupid'. *Commentary,* June 1994.

Gannicott, Ken *Taking Education Seriously: A Reform Program for Australia's Schools*. Centre for Independent Studies, St Leonards, NSW, 1997.

Gintis, Herbert (reviewing John E. Chubb and Terry M. Moe *Politics, Markets and America's Schools*. Brookings Institution, Washington, DC, 1990). *British Journal of Sociology of Education, Review Symposium* 12(3), 1991.

Goodson, Ivor *School Subjects and Curriculum Change*. Croom Helm, London, 1983.

Green, Anthony (reviewing John E. Chubb and Terry M. Moe *Politics, Markets and America's Schools*. Brookings Institution, Washington, DC, 1990) *British Journal of Sociology of Education* 12(3), 1991, 390.

Halfon, Robert *Corporate Irresponsibility: Is Business Appeasing Anti-Business Activists?* Social Affairs Unit, London, 1998.

Hall, Stuart 'Some Politically Incorrect Pathways Through PC' in Sarah Dunant (ed.) *The War of the Words: The Political Correctness Debate*. Virago, London, 1994.

Hayek, Friedrich von *The Road to Serfdom*. Routledge and Kegan Paul, London, 1944.

Hayek, Friedrich von 'The Use of Knowledge in Society'. *American Economic Review* XXXV(4), September 1945.

Hayek, Friedrich von 'Economics and Knowledge', in *Individualism and Economic Order*. Routledge, London, 1948.

Hayek, Friedrich von *The Constitution of Liberty*. Routledge and Kegan Paul, London, 1960.

Hirsch, E. D. *Cultural Literacy: What Every American Needs to Know*. Vintage, New York, 1988.

Hirsch, E. D. Jr *The Schools We Need and Why We Don't Have Them*. Doubleday, New York, 1996.

Hirschman, Alfred O. *Rival Views of Market Society and Other Recent Essays*. Viking, New York, 1987.

Horowitz, Irving Louis 'The Decomposition of Sociology'. *Academic Questions*, Spring 1992.

Hughes, Robert *Culture of Complaint: the Fraying of America*. Harvill, London, 1994.

Jaggar, Alison *Feminist Politics and Human Nature*. Rowman and Allanheld, Totowa, NJ, 1983.

James, Harold *The German Slump: Politics and Economics, 1924–1936*. Clarendon Press, Oxford, 1986.

Johnson, Daniel 'Enter the New Nihilists'. *Daily Telegraph*, 7 November 1998, p. 24.

Johnson, Paul *Modern Times: A History of the World from the 1920s to the 1990s*. Phoenix, London, 1996.

Killpatrick, William *Why Johnny Can't Tell Right from Wrong*. Simon and Schuster, New York, 1993.

Kimball, Roger *Tenured Radicals*. Harper and Row, New York, 1990.

Kirzner, Israel M. *How Markets Work: Disequilibrium, Entrepreneurship and Discovery*. Hobart Paper No. 133, Insitute for Economic Affairs, London, 1997.

Koestler, Arthur *Darkness at Noon*. Penguin, Harmondsworth, 1964.

Kors, Alan Charles and Silvergate, Harvey *The Shadow University: The Betrayal of Liberty on America's Campuses.* Free Press, New York, 1998.

Kramer, Rita *Ed School Follies: The Miseducation of America's Teachers.* Free Press, New York, 1991.

Landes, David *The Wealth and Poverty of Nations.* Little, Brown, Boston, 1998.

Lane, David *Politics and Society in the USSR.* Martin Robertson, London, 1978.

Lasch, Christopher *The Revolt of the Elites.* Norton, New York, 1994.

Lieberman, Myron *Privatisation and Educational Choice.* Saint Martin's Press, New York, 1989.

Lieberman, Myron, Haar, Charlene and Troy, Leo *The NEA and the AFT: Teachers' Unions in Power and Politics.* Pro-Active Publications, Rockport, MA, 1994.

Marks, John *An Anatomy of Failure: Standards in English Schools for 1997.* Memorandum, Social Market Foundation London, September 1998.

Marsland, David 'Vast Horizons, Meagre Visions' in Digby Anderson *et al. Breaking the Spell of the Welfare State.* Social Affairs Unit, London, 1981.

Marsland, David *Seeds of Bankruptcy: Sociological Bias Against Business and Freedom.* Claridge, London, 1988.

Marsland, David *Welfare or Welfare State: Contradictions and Dilemmas in Social Policies.* Macmillan, Basingstoke, 1996.

McGowan, William 'A Politically Incorrect Study of PC'. *Wall Street Journal,* 4 January 1995.

McKinstry, Leo 'The Emptiness of Labour's New Policy on Marriage'. *Sunday Telegraph*, 1 November 1998, p. 35.

McKinstry, Leo 'Macpherson Was Just a Useful Idiot'. *Sunday Telegraph,* 28 February 1999.

MORI (for the Independent Schools Information Service) *Attitudes to Independent Schools.* MORI, London, October 1998.

Mises, Ludwig von *Socialism: An Economic and Sociological Analysis*. Jonathan Cape, London, 1936.

Murray, Charles *Losing Ground: American Social Policy, 1950–1980*. Basic Books, New York, 1984.

Murray, Charles *The Underclass: The Crisis Deepens*. Institute of Economic Affairs, London, 1994.

Norcross, Lawrence 'The Classics: Small Latin and Less Greek' in Dennis O'Keeffe (ed.) *The Wayward Curriculum*. Social Affairs Unit, London, 1986.

O'Hear, Anthony *Nonsense about Nature*. Social Affairs Unit, London, 1997.

O'Keeffe, Dennis J. 'Profit and Control : the Bowles and Gintis Thesis.' *Journal of Curriculum Studies*, September 1978.

O'Keeffe, Dennis 'Market Capitalism and Nationalised School' in Davies, B. (ed.) *The State of Schooling, Educational Analysis*, Spring 1981.

O'Keeffe, Dennis 'The Name of the Game is Weber.' *Education Today* 36(2), 1986.

O'Keeffe, Dennis J. *The Wayward Elite*. Adam Smith Institute, London, 1990.

O'Keeffe, Dennis 'Diligence Abandoned' in Digby Anderson (ed.) *The Loss of Virtue*. Social Affairs Unit, London, 1992.

O'Keeffe, Dennis 'Multiculturalism and Cultural Literacy' in Geoff Partington (ed.) *Cultural Literacy. International Journal of Social Education* 9(1), Spring/Summer 1994.

O'Keeffe, D. J. (Dennis) *Truancy in English Secondary Schools*. HMSO, London, 1994.

O'Keeffe, Dennis 'The Philistine Trap' in Ralph Segalman (ed.) *Reclaiming the Family*. Paragon House, New York, 1998.

Orwell, George *1984,* with an introduction by Julian Symons. David Campbell, London, 1992.

Orwell, Sonia and Angus, Ian (eds) *Orwell, The Collected Essays* etc. Vol. 3, 'As I Please'. Penguin, Harmondsworth, 1968.

O'Sullivan, John 'The Next Great Threat to Liberal Democracy'. *Daily Telegraph,* 8 March 1999.

Peters, Richard S. *Ethics and Education*. Allen and Unwin, London, 1966.

Phillips, Melanie 'Illiberal Liberalism' in Sarah Dunant (ed.) *The War of the Words*. Virago, London, 1994.

Phillips, Melanie *All Must Have Prizes*. Little, Brown, Boston, 1996, pp. 119–206.

Popper, Karl *The Open Society and its Enemies*. Routledge, London, 1962.

Radnitzky, Gerard 'Sorting Social Systems' in Gerard Radnitzky (ed.) *Values and the Social Order* Vol. 3: *Voluntary versus Coercive Orders*. Avebury, Aldershot, 1997.

Schumpeter, Joseph A. *Capitalism, Socialism and Democracy*. Allen and Unwin, London, 1942.

Schwarzschild Leopold *The Red Prussian: The Life and Legend of Karl Marx*. Pickwick, London, 1986.

Scruton, Roger *Modern Philosophy*. Sinclair Stevenson, London, 1994.

Scruton, Roger 'Opening Fire in the Real Culture Wars'. *The Times*, 4 January 1996.

Scruton, Roger *An Intelligent Person's Guide to Modern Culture*. Duckworth, London, 1998.

Segalman, Ralph 'The Underclass Re-Visited: Causes and Solutions' in David Marsland (ed.) *Work and Employment*. Paragon, New York, 1994.

Seldon, Arthur *The Riddle of the Voucher: An Inquiry into the Obstacles to Introducing Choice and Competition in State Schools*. Institute of Economic Affairs, London, 1986.

Seldon, Arthur (ed.) *Reprivatising Welfare After the Lost Century*. Institute of Economic Affairs, London, 1996.

Seldon, Arthur *The Dilemma of Democracy: The Political Economics of Over-Government*. Hobart Paper 136, Institute of Economic Affairs, London, 1998.

Shafarevich, Igor *The Socialist Phenomenon* with an introduction by Alexander Solzhenitsyn. Harper and Row, New York, 1990.

Shanker, A. 'Where We Stand'. *New Republic,* 4 November 1986.

Shatz, Marshall 'Jan Waclaw Machajski: The Conspiracy of the Intellectuals'. *Survey,* January 1967.

Silone, Ignazio. *Fontamara.* Dent, London, 1985.

Solzhenitsyn, Alexander 'The Relentless Cult of Novelty'. *Salisbury Review,* September 1993.

Syall, Meera *PC: GLC* in Sarah Dunant (ed.) *The War of the Words: The Political Correctness Debate.* Virago, London, 1994.

Tooley, James *Education Without the State.* Institute of Economic Affairs, London, 1996.

Tooley, James *The Global Education Industry.* Institute of Economic Affairs, London, 1999.

West, E. G. 'Education Without the State' in Arthur Seldon (ed.) *Reprivatising Welfare After the Lost Century.* Institute of Economic Affairs, London, 1996.

White, John *The Aims of Education Restated.* Routledge and Kegan Paul, London, 1982.

Williams, Gareth and Woodhall, Maureen *Independent Further Education.* Policy Studies Institute, London, 1979.

Wilson, John K. *The Myth of Political Correctness* Duke University Press, Durham, NC, 1995.

Yates, Steven *Civil Wrongs: What Went Wrong With Affirmative Action.* Institute for Contemporary Studies Press, San Francisco, CA, 1994.

Young, M. F. D. *Knowledge and Control.* Collier Macmillan, London, 1971.

Glossary of non-economic terms

Antinomianism: in modern usage this means hostility to settled laws and traditions of culture, morality and custom.

Ascription: differentiation of people in terms of traits over which they have no control, e.g. race, sex or caste.

Epistemic: concerning knowledge.

Gnosis: a doctrine claiming special knowledge and understanding of mysteries impenetrable to the uninitiated.

Hypertrophy: excessive and uncontrolled growth.

Marxisant: intellectually fellow-travelling with Marxism.

Nihilism: the denial of any ultimate truth or moral order.

Particularism: the claim that individuals are constituted by particular characteristics, e.g. race, sex or culture, rather than universal humanity.

Praxis: originally a Marxist term meaning a union of theory and practice, hence now any institutionalised theory.

Psychologism: an argument reducing human behaviour to purely pyschological causes.

Rightsology: the overextended and intemperate campaigning for human and other rights.

113

Sectoral socialism: any public sector activity in market economies, with the additional characteristic of institutionalised egalitarianism.

Separatism: any doctrine favouring separation between groups, e.g. on sex or race lines.

Sociologism: an argument reducing behaviour to purely sociological terms.

Victimology: a disposition to see oppressors and victims everywhere.

The Global Education Industry

Lessons from Private Education in Developing Countries

James Tooley

Changes in private education now underway in the developing world could have a dramatic impact on the lives of millions worldwide.

Drawing on examples from Argentina, Brazil, Colombia, India, Indonesia, Peru, Romania, Russia, South Africa, Zimbabwe and other countries, Professor Tooley gives a snapshot of private education that may surprise many readers: contrary to expectations, the private education sector is large in the countries studied, it is innovative, and it is not the exclusive domain of the wealthy. The author challenges the conventional wisdom that private education in developing countries fosters greater social and economic inequality; he points out that such education often provides creative social responsibility programmes, subsidised places, and student loan schemes.

James Tooley identifies the factors that impede or facilitate the development of the private education sector in various countries, focusing on the regulatory regimes that may impinge upon private education.

Finally, he considers the ways in which the existence of an innovative private education sector could influence education policy as practised by international agencies and national governments. He concludes with a 'modest proposal' for how for-profit education enterprises could play an important role in promoting equitable development.

The Institute of Economic Affairs
2 Lord North Street, Westminster, London SW1P 3LB
Telephone: 0171 799 3745 Facsimile: 0171 799 2137
E-mail: iea@iea.org.uk Internet: http://www.iea.org.uk

£8.00

ISBN 0-255 36475-X

Teacher Education in England and Wales

Geoffrey Partington

Geoffrey Partington places within its historical context the take-over of teacher education in Britain during the late 1960s and the 1970s by the then 'New Left'. He examines attempts made after 1979 by Conservative governments to repair the severe damage inflicted by the New Left on teacher education and British education as a whole. These included 'bottom-up' policies which widened entry into teaching, but the emphasis was on 'top-down' policies, culminating in a national curriculum for teacher education comparable to that devised for the school system.

Teacher educators interviewed by Partington in 1997 often criticised Conservative policies in general, but held that their own courses were much better than in 1979. Partington agrees that closer co-operation between schools and higher education was secured and initial teacher training improved in efficiency and became more sensitive to actual teaching conditions. However, he regrets the sharp reduction of time devoted to theoretical studies of any sort and urges that the answer to bad educational ideas should be better educational ideas, not attempts to make teaching a practical activity based almost entirely on classroom experience.

That 'New Labour' has not reversed but extended Conservative 'top-down' policies appears to some to be evidence that the Conservatives had the balance right. Partington argues to the contrary that long-term substantial improvement can only be achieved by significantly freeing-up teacher education and the education system as a whole.

The Institute of Economic Affairs
2 Lord North Street, Westminster, London SW1P 3LB
Telephone: 0171 799 3745   Facsimile: 0171 799 2137
E-mail: iea@iea.org.uk   Internet: http://www.iea.org.uk   ISBN 0-255 36476-8

£12.00